lonely planet

WASHINGTON, DC
ENCOUNTER

ADAM KARLIN

Washington, DC Encounter

Published by Lonely Planet Publications Pty Ltd
ABN 36 005 607 983

Australia Head Office,
Locked Bag 1, Footscray, Vic 3011
☎ 03 8379 8000 fax 03 8379 8111
talk2us@lonelyplanet.com.au

USA 150 Linden St, Oakland, CA 94607
☎ 510 250 6400
toll free 800 275 8555
fax 510 893 8572
info@lonelyplanet.com

UK 2nd fl, 186 City Rd
London EC1V 2NT
☎ 020 7106 2100 fax 020 7106 2101
go@lonelyplanet.co.uk

This title was commissioned in Lonely Planet's Oakland office, and was produced by: **Commissioning Editor** Jennye Garibaldi **Coordinating Editors** Michelle Bennett, Laura Gibb, Kate Whitfield **Coordinating Cartographer** David Kemp **Coordinating Layout Designer** Frank Deim **Senior Editor** Helen Christinis **Managing Editor** Brigitte Ellemor **Managing Cartographers** David Connolly, Alison Lyall **Managing Layout Designers** Laura Jane, Indra Kilfoyle **Assisting Editors** Daniel Corbett, Rosie Nicholson **Assisting Cartographer** Eve Kelly **Cover Designer** Katy Murenu **Project Manager** Craig Kilburn **Thanks to** Lucy Birchley, Ross Butler, Catherine Craddock-Carrillo, Heather Dickson, Joshua Geoghegan, Emily K Wolman

ISBN 978 1 74179 604 9

Printed through Colorcraft Ltd, Hong Kong.
Printed in China.

Acknowledgement Washington Metropolitan Area Transit Authority © 2008.

HOW TO USE THIS BOOK

Color-Coding & Maps

Color-coding is used for symbols on maps and in the text that they relate to (eg all eating venues on the maps and in the text are given a green knife and fork symbol). Each neighborhood also gets its own color, and this is used down the edge of the page and throughout that neighborhood section.

Shaded yellow areas on the maps denote 'areas of interest' – for their historical significance, their attractive architecture or their great bars and restaurants. We encourage you to head to these areas and just start exploring!

Send us your feedback We love to hear from readers – your comments help make our books better. We read every word you send us, and we always guarantee that your feedback goes straight to the appropriate authors. The most useful submissions are rewarded with a free book. To send us your updates and find out about Lonely Planet events, newsletters and travel news, visit our award-winning website: ***lonelyplanet.com/contact***.

Note: We may edit, reproduce and incorporate your comments in Lonely Planet products such as guidebooks, websites and digital products, so let us know if you don't want your comments reproduced or your name acknowledged. For a copy of our privacy policy visit ***lonelyplanet.com/privacy***.

ADAM KARLIN

Dirty secret: Adam, while born in Washington, DC (George Washington Hospital, 1980, to be exact), grew up in...Maryland. DC residents may now cringe. And he barely visited the capital beyond field trips before he lit out to see the world, aspiring Lonely Planet–author style, working as a journalist and editor in Thailand, Laos, India, Sri Lanka, Vietnam, Australia, Argentina and England, plus as a reporter at a fair few newspapers state-side, including a stint at community newspapers in Prince George's County, which borders the capital. It was during this period that Adam spent more and more time in his backyard, both learning it and loving it. Today Lonely Planet sends him as far afield as Kenya, Cameroon, the Andaman Islands and Malaysia, but he still loves getting to explore Washington, a city that speaks both to his love of the international and his inner Maryland redneck.

ADAM'S THANKS

Thanks to the friends and family and new contacts who always make Washington feel like home to this itinerant wanderer. In particular, thank you local voices (Chris, John and Kenny) and Jordan, Maria and Jessie, who were invaluable research 'aides' – and more importantly, friends – in the winter of 2008.

Our readers Many thanks to the travelers who wrote to us with helpful hints, useful advice and interesting anecdotes. Brooke Bennett, Stefanie Bode, Edwin De Voogd, Jeruen Dery, Will Gibbons, Gina Gomez, Ben Hindman, Jong Hyun Jang, Irving Levinson, John Lockwood, Rebecca Menes, Rodney Miles, Heather Monell, Megan Peniston-Bird, Marcus Roper, Lillian Rosen, Tina Seashore, Craig Smith, Carolyn Stachowski, Paul Summers, Karen Vock, Tony Wheeler.

Cover photograph Balloons celebrating a new American dawn over the Capitol dome (p43); Joseph Sohm, Corbis. **Internal photographs** p13, p125 courtesy of the Smithsonian Institution; p17 Jeff Hutchens, Getty. All photographs by Lonely Planet Images, and by Jason Colston p20, p29, p78, p82, p85, p90, p93, p102, p114, p122, p126; Justin Mathews p13, p51, p53, p57, p59, p60, p107, p109, p110, p130, p133, p141; as well as Rob Blakers p121; Richard Cummins p25, p48, p72, p100, p125; Lee Foster p10, p19, p26 (bottom), p37, p39, p66; Greg Gawlowski p4, p6 (bottom), p16; Rick Gerharter p21, p137; Dan Herrick p6 (top), p15, p26 (top), p30, p65, p118, p132; Dennis Johnson p8, p22, p40; John Neubauer p143; Witold Skrypczak p95; Lawrence Worcester p18.

An unmissable memorial to the first president: the Washington Monument (p41)

CONTENTS

Why is our travel information the best in the world? It's simple: our authors are passionate, dedicated travelers. They don't take freebies in exchange for positive coverage so you can be sure the advice you're given is impartial. They travel widely to all the popular spots, and off the beaten track. They don't research using just the internet or phone. They discover new places not included in any other guidebook. They personally visit thousands of hotels, restaurants, palaces, trails, galleries, temples and more. They speak with dozens of locals every day to make sure you get the kind of insider knowledge only a local could tell you. They take pride in getting all the details right, and in telling it how it is. Think you can do it? Find out how at **lonelyplanet.com**.

VE SWORN
WE HOLD THESE TRUTHS TO B
EVIDENT: THAT ALL MEN ARE CR
THAT THEY ARE ENDOWED

THIS IS WASHINGTON, DC

Like few cities in America, Washington is both a beneficiary and a victim of perception.

One version comprises marble, monuments and museums in the shadow of the Capitol dome. Great restaurants, wild clubs. More culture – the Smithsonian, the Kennedy Center, the Folger – than a city this size deserves, plus a National Mall that's the front yard and public podium of the American people.

The other version of Washington is where too many wake up to a morning-after hangover of the American dream, transplants and aristocrats float above the fray, and the federal government seems to turn a blind eye to its own home.

Which is the real Washington? All of the above. Yet the two-cities-in-one stereotype limits this great town. Like the nation she governs, DC is defined by her compromises, not her extremes. And conversations about where that nation is headed occur here with more frequency and passion than anywhere else in America.

Contrary to popular belief, this conversation occurs among out-of-town politicos *and* folks, as they say here, from around the way. The ones who remember Danny Ferry's fast break at DeMatha and Mark the Ripper at RFK. People who know Kissinger preferred Chinese at Yengching Palace before it closed, even though Full Kee does better duck. Guys who would never eat on the Mall, but know it well enough to recommend Constitution Gardens for the sunset (17th and Constitution, by the way).

When it comes to politics, DC's homegrown will argue you under the table. That's the soul of this city: not divisions or iconography, but a population that's as intellectually stimulating as any Manhattan dinner party, and as comfortably down-home as mom's mac 'n' cheese (which our soul-food joints cook best).

But don't take our word for it. Real Washingtonians might be opinionated as hell, but they're also twice as warm, so come visit, and see a global capital that's local enough to love.

Top An icon of American jazz: Bohemian Caverns (p87) **Bottom** A bronzed third president standing proud at the Thomas Jefferson Memorial (p40)

>HIGHLIGHTS

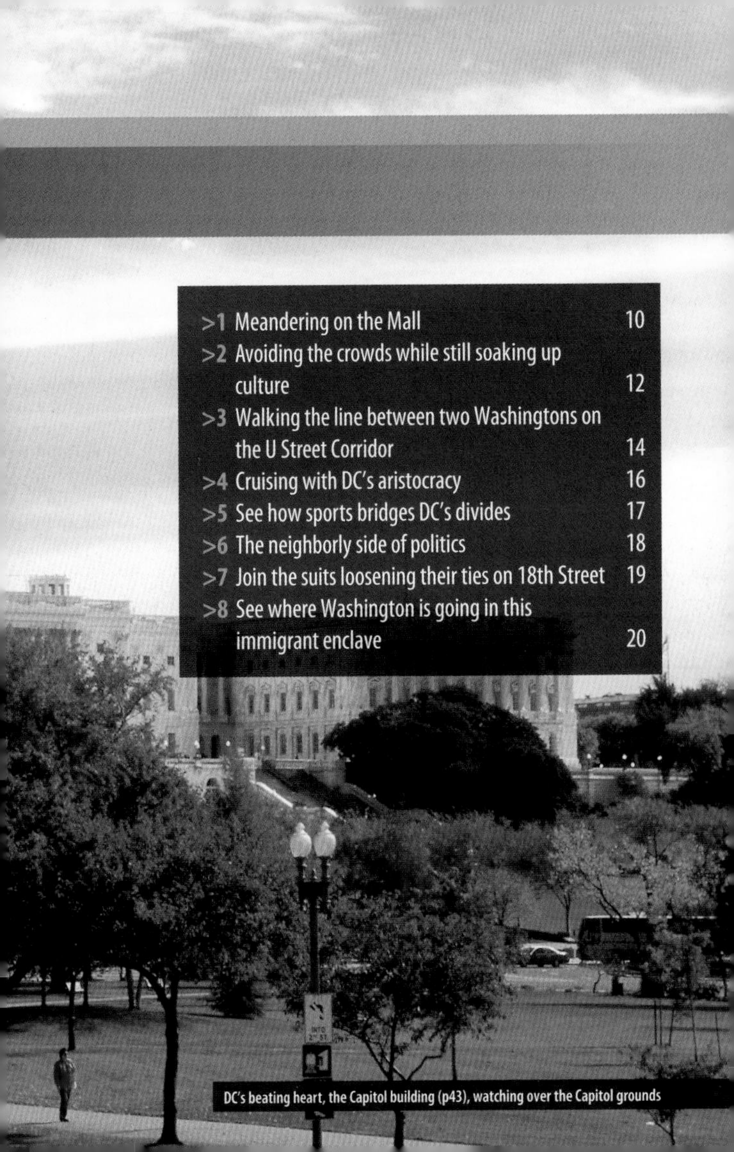

DC's beating heart, the Capitol building (p43), watching over the Capitol grounds

>1 NATIONAL MALL

MEANDERING ON THE MALL

We love Washington, DC for what lies beneath her majestic facade, but if beauty is skin deep, the District is still pretty hot thanks to her most recognizable landmarks. Whatever else DC is, she's a capital first, and as such is dotted with the most potent symbols of the American narrative. Gleaming buildings, memorials and sculptures are scattered throughout town, but reach their greatest concentration here.

These icons combine with museums that house the country's knowledge, monuments to heroes and a 1.9-mile scabby lawn to form the great public green of the American consciousness: the National Mall, heart of not just Washington, but perhaps the USA as well.

Whether you're a skeptic of or fervent believer in the American dream, that story informs the nation's vision of itself, and you can't find more concrete symbols of this abstract ideal than the towering structures that frame the Mall. Wandering from the Capitol dome (p43) to the Lincoln Memorial (p37; pictured above) is like entering a cathedral: simultaneously humbling and inspiring.

And in many ways the Mall is essentially a house of worship: a secular place of pilgrimage for those who profess faith in democracy, and a patriotic temple to the American experiment. The deities this country enshrines are all here. The real potential for growth, change and a better life feels evident, and the value of intangibles such as freedom and liberty obvious, in written records from the Library of Congress (p46) to the National Archives (p38).

Yet the Mall is not just overwhelmingly grand. When an Ultimate team member from Arlington yells, 'Little help!' after they toss their Frisbee into a Punjabi family picnic, or an Angolan couple takes pictures of Bob and Fran from Indiana in front of the Washington Monument (p41), or a Polaroid of a newborn underwritten by 'I wish you could have met her, dad' is laid under the dark mirror of the Vietnam Veterans Memorial (p40), you realize the act of experiencing the Mall is made up of small intimate moments, which are somehow very accessible amid all the grandeur.

Visiting the Mall for the sake of the Mall itself, rather than any one individual museum or monument, takes the better part of a day. Come here in a mood as reflective as the pool in front of the Lincoln Memorial, and prepare yourself for a walk through, with and into American identity.

>2 UNDERRATED MUSEUMS

AVOIDING THE CROWDS WHILE STILL SOAKING UP CULTURE

Washington, DC has one of the world's great concentrations of museums, most of them free. Unfortunately, many of them are also crowded, especially on weekends when, thanks to armies of small children, spots such as the National Air & Space Museum transform into the Zoo of Chaos.

But there are so many museums here, you're bound to find something that tickles your cultural fancy that's also sheltered from the heaving masses.

The National Museum of African Art (p38) contains an excellent, if West Africa–heavy, collection of both traditional and modern art from the continent. The latter is a nice reminder that the creativity of Africa isn't limited to masks and drums, often a limitation of similar institutions. Almost adjacent are the Freer and Sackler Galleries (p36). These quiet, contemplative chambers house reams of elegant Asian art; it's the sort of place where a Tibetan demon stares angrily across the room at the serene smile of a Gandharan Buddha, who meditates in the shadow of Hindu temple lintels that are arranged opposite Chinese silk scroll paintings and Japanese screens. The collection of Whistler originals is somehow not as incongruous as you might think – there are many lines to be drawn (figuratively) between the American master's impressionism and the abstract aesthetics of nearby Zen masters.

Surprisingly few visitors to the Mall discover the peace of the sculpture garden outside of the Hirshhorn Museum (p36). If you've been wearing yourself out with long trudges across and through the nation's front yard, consider taking a break here among works by Rodin, Jean Arp and others. The garden is best visited in spring and early summer.

You have to pay to enter and it's worth it: the Corcoran Gallery (p90) is the largest nonfederal museum in Washington, DC, an excellent repository of American art and a beautiful building besides. The traveling exhibitions in particular have a reputation for rivaling anything on display in the Smithsonian institutions, which is no small accomplishment.

Finally, while they're not underrated per se, the upper floors of the Smithsonian American Art Museum & National Portrait Gallery (p56; pictured) are rarely packed with crowds (probably because there's so much museum in the lower levels). The magnificent top floor is actually the grand hall of the old US Patent Office and is an exhibition in itself, but there are still countless photos, paintings and sculptures to explore, including an incredible three-*extra*-story annex crowning the whole affair.

>3 U STREET

WALKING THE LINE BETWEEN TWO WASHINGTONS ON THE U STREET CORRIDOR

In 1968, U and 14th St NW was the epicenter of riots that followed Martin Luther King Jr's assassination and tore the capital apart. These days, the same intersection has evolved into an epicenter of gentrification that's centrally located amidst some of the city's best restaurants and bars. For the city's young professionals, U St is a godsend, a neighborhood that offers what many call 'affordable lifestyle' (you know: yoga, ethnic food, wine, Pilates, vintage shopping), which was once largely restricted to the District's deep and/or connected pockets. Here, all of the above is affordable and hip.

A local tells us the biggest change to U St over the past two decades is this: 'Well, white people jog there now.' But to be fair, white people – and brown and black – are doing a lot more than running through the heart of what was once DC's version of Harlem. They're also shopping in boutiques such as Nana (p84), boozing in bars like Stetson's (p87), gallery browsing in artist co-ops like Dekka (p83) and eating everything from upscale chicken and waffles at Crème (p85) to mustard-and-chili-drenched half smokes at Ben's (p84; pictured right).

Development is always a double-edged sword, and there are many who believe U St is the precursor of a pattern that will repeat across the city: neighborhoods sacrificing their character to gain yuppie appeal. But the area's transformation has partly been led by black businesspeople who have been revitalizing the 'hood and resurrecting black institutions such as the excellent jazz club at Bohemian Caverns (p87). There's 'scene' here now, and the folks behind and benefiting from it are a multicolored cast, a reminder that this once was, and is now, the sort of place that inspired geniuses like Duke Ellington.

The drama of old and new Washington is exemplified by Ben's Chili Bowl – a symbol of Old School DC if ever there was one – now located mere blocks from the fresh, clean and bohemian Busboys & Poets (p84). While the two businesses may seem physically and culturally worlds apart, they're both black-owned and committed to DC's black community, which is, perhaps imperfectly but certainly inevitably, integrating into the new Washington on the U St line.

CHILI
SMOKES
Ben's
Chili Bowl
CHILI
BURGER
A WASHINGTON LANDMARK SINCE 19
BEN'S
Chili Bowl
BEN'S
OPEN
Chili
SMOKES
Chili
BURGERS

>4 GEORGETOWN

CRUISING WITH DC'S ARISTOCRACY

Georgetown is the name of both one of the premier universities in the world and a neighborhood that has long been the seat of Washingtonian royalty: a brick-and-old-stone tangle of leafy avenues, cobbled alleyways, diplomats walking their kids to prep school and professors deconstructing experimental theater over glasses of merlot. But come Thursday night, this neighborhood sublimates all of the above and becomes, basically, a big river of boiling hormones.

There's a distinctly upper-class crust to the Georgetown scene that sets it apart. Whether you love or loathe the local nightlife, the fact is you may never get the chance to see so much American Old Money and aristocracy acting the fool in bars such as Mr Smith's (p79) and Mie N Yu (p78) outside of Harvard Sq.

Of course there's a reason the moneyed classes love this 'hood, although the appeal extends to anyone who hikes here. Dining is romantic (JFK proposed to Jackie at Martin's; see p78) and ethnically diverse, and sometimes, surprisingly affordable. Georgetown is the Sigmund Freud of DC's retail therapy, so shopaholics rejoice at boutiques like Relish (p74). And the historic veneer of the neighborhood is well preserved – the Old Stone House (p73) is the oldest building in DC – making it a magical place for a stroll in the early evening, as long as you avoid the traffic-clogged main drag of M St.

>5 CATCHING A GAME

SEE HOW SPORTS BRIDGES DC'S DIVIDES

Popular wisdom holds that in America, baseball is embraced by the Northeast, football by the South and basketball by African Americans. Washington incorporates people from every one of these demographics, and no one in this town limits themselves to any one game.

DC loves sports. For locals who resent the way New Yorkers, Baltimoreans and Philadelphians categorize their town as a city populated by transplants, game days are a reminder that competitive – and community – roots here run deep. For actual transplants, watching teams like the Nationals at Nationals Stadium (p46) or the Redskins at FedExField (http://fedex.com/us/sports/fedexfield) or in a Capitol Hill pub like the Hawk & Dove (p51) provides a sense of grounding and neutral territory where Senate staffers from across the aisle can discuss anything besides politics. For immigrants, a day at the game, any game, is an introduction to their new homeland's strange traditions. It can also be a way of introducing new traditions to the American saga: an indelible DC image is the sight of a private-school kid from Bethesda gleefully hugging a Salvadoran construction worker in the stands of a DC United soccer game at RFK (p53).

>6 CAPITOL HILL

THE NEIGHBORLY SIDE OF POLITICS

OK, off the bat, we'll warn you that Capitol Hill – the neighborhood, not the complex of the Capitol dome (p43), Supreme Court (p48) and Library of Congress (p46) – is not packed with obvious sightseeing destinations, although with that said, you're only a skip away from the federal landmarks listed above (which are all, needless to say, awesome).

Instead, what makes Capitol Hill appealing is its well-executed blend of DC neighborliness and the city's political class. Washington is jokingly called 'Hollywood for Ugly People,' thanks to the high concentration of political types here, and many of these 'stars' (who are hardly all unattractive, thank you very much) can be seen here walking their dogs weekday evenings on Mass Ave NE.

They're strolling by some of the city's most attractive old row houses, which are largely inhabited by families that are several-generations-deep steeped in DC. And come the weekend, everyone, from the neighborhood watch to presidential chiefs of staff, goes to Eastern Market (p43) to buy flowers, produce, paintings and the best oyster sandwiches in town. The most political address in the city is proof that a sense of community remains strong in a capital whose population tends to shift with elections every four years.

>7 ADAMS MORGAN/DUPONT CIRCLE

JOIN THE SUITS LOOSENING THEIR TIES ON 18TH STREET

When it comes to going out, Adams Morgan and Dupont Circle have been the kings of the DC scene for decades, and while interesting restaurants, bars and clubs are constantly cropping up in Columbia Heights and along H St, this is still the eye of Washington's nightlife hurricane.

But it's not just about having fun here – although there's plenty of that to be had. Adams Morgan is still a muddy, mixed-race entrepôt of Ethiopians, Ghanaians, Sudanese and, from the other side of the Atlantic, Salvadorans, Nicaraguans and Guatemalans. Streaking through this rich cultural mix is 18th St NW, which is by far the busiest strip in the capital on a weekend night. Love it or hate it, you haven't done DC till you've wandered up this way for a late-night empanada or jumbo slice (p109).

Dupont Circle (p62; pictured above) is more civilized, if just as enjoyable. Here, ethnic diversity takes a back seat to sexual liberation; this is the heart of DC's strong gay community. It's also ground zero for dozens of embassies and their staff, various think tanks and a café culture birthed by the interaction of literally thousands of diplomats, research associates and international institution types.

>8 COLUMBIA HEIGHTS

SEE WHERE WASHINGTON IS GOING IN THIS IMMIGRANT ENCLAVE

The most exciting area of any city is its edge, that spot where cheap rents, immigrants, artists and innovators all seem to congregate. It was U St last decade, and in this cycle it's looking like Columbia Heights and Northeast DC beyond will take the crown.

Old DC is still very much here, detectable in an argument over jazz in the Raven (p102; pictured above), a dive that manages to put fun and grit into one powerful shot of nightlife goodness. But said bar sits on Mt Pleasant Ave (p98), where members of DC's Salvadoran community do their shopping, raise their children and integrate into the newest face of the American experience. This sometimes has delicious results – see what happens when Central and North America come together in cafés such as Dos Gringos (p100).

Among this mix of new arrivals and natives are entrepreneurs thriving off the energy of an area where anything seems possible. Down Upshur St from great DC diner the Hitching Post (p101) is the slick but hardly soulless coffee shop and Eastern European/ Scandinavian restaurant W Domku (p101), as incongruous as a Viking in residential Northeast DC – except someone gave this Viking a hip interior and a healthy respect for the neighborhood he's settled in. Would that all Norse invasions were so peaceful.

>CALENDAR

Shake a cherry blossom tree, unfurl your rainbow flag, practice the Chinese lion dance and watch a president get sworn in – that's how years are passed in Washington, DC, a city that certainly doesn't lack for ceremonies. There's more happening in town than those listings marked on the official city calendar. For more on events, festivals and fetes, check out www.washingtoncitypaper.com, http://washington.dc.eventguide.com and www.culturaltourismdc.org, or walk down the National Mall and find a protest, parade or rally that might make this date go down in history, even if it hasn't officially done so yet.

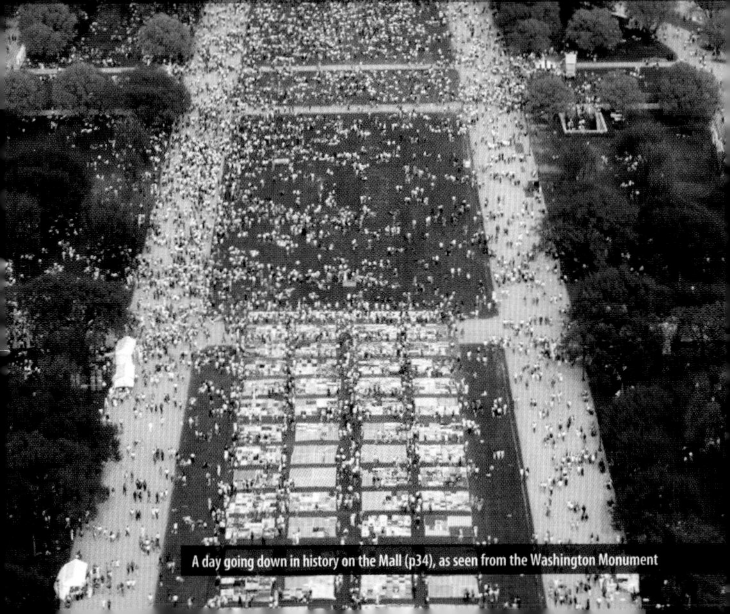

A day going down in history on the Mall (p34), as seen from the Washington Monument

JANUARY

Chinese New Year

☎ 202-638-1041

Centered on Chinatown (duh) and led by a lion dance, lots of street food and a few firecrackers. Late January/early February.

Presidential Inauguration

Held every four years. Try to catch the pomp and circumstance that accompanies these peaceful power transitions. January 20.

FEBRUARY

Black History Month

Lectures, plays, performances and readings occur throughout town; for up-to-date listings, check with the Anacostia Community Museum (http://anacostia.si.edu).

Washington DC International Wine & Food Festival

☎ 800-343-1174; www.wine-expos.com/wine/dc

Local and celebrity chefs gather and get all epicurean for two days. Expect good food, good booze and good times.

MARCH

National Cherry Blossom Festival

http://nationalcherryblossomfestival.org

Washington looks her best when 3000 Japanese cherry trees blanket early spring with flurries of pink petals. Late March to early April.

Pretty in pink: Thomas Jefferson Memorial (p40)

Smithsonian Kite Festival

www.kitefestival.org

The skies above the Mall fill up with silk, paper and plenty of colorful bunting on the last Saturday of March.

APRIL

Filmfest DC

www.filmfestdc.org

Cutting-edge cinema by domestic and international directors is showcased at Washington's biggest film festival. Ten days towards the end of the month.

White House Easter Egg Roll

☎ 202-456-7041; www.whitehouse.gov/easter

Kids celebrate spring on the White House South Lawn for free – it's a 130-year tradition. Monday after Easter.

MAY

DC Black Pride

www.dcblackpride.org

The nation's largest black pride festival is a celebration, a commemoration and a can't-miss if you're in town for the lovely spring season.

Passport DC

www.passportdc.org

One of DC's newest and more innovative festivals, with many embassies throwing their doors open to the public for two weeks.

JUNE

Capital Pride

☎ 202-905-2785; www.capitalpride.org

Washington's biggest gay festival attracts the usual Village People party atmosphere, plus queer activists, artists and acts.

Folklife

www.folklife.si.edu

The Smithsonian hosts original, eclectic pavilions of 'living culture' themes on the Mall, ranging from Buddhism to space exploration to Wales.

SUMMER IN THE CITY

Summer nights are sultry and set aside for concerts, most of which are free, that are held throughout the city from Memorial Day to the Labor Day weekend.

Free concerts are held at the National Zoo (p112) every Thursday evening. The National Sculpture Garden at 7th and Constitution Ave NW, features Jazz in the Garden every Friday night in summer from 7pm, and the marine corps, air force, army and navy bands perform on the steps of the Capitol on alternating days in summer.

JULY

Independence Day

It's so hot you could bottle the humid air as 'Muggy No 5' – and for all that, there's no better time to be here. Celebrate Christmas at the North Pole, right? As with July 4 here: outdoor parties aplenty and a fireworks display that makes the Mall magic.

SEPTEMBER

Adams Morgan Festival

www.adamsmorgandayfestival.com

It's a neighborhood festival – the city's biggest – and an international one notable for kick-ass street food, too. Weekend after Labor Day.

FARMERS MARKET MADNESS

Farmers markets are very popular in the nation's capital – Washingtonians are as obsessed with locally sourced produce as the rest. Fresh goodies are for sale every Saturday and Sunday at the Eastern Market (p43) from 8am until 4pm. The official DC Farmers Market is open on a year-round basis from 7am to 5:30pm Tuesday, till 6pm Saturday and till 2pm Sunday at 1309 5th St NE. If you're in Dupont Circle, stalls sell from 9am until 1pm on Sunday (from 10am January to March) on the 1500 block of 20th St NW, between Q St & Massachusetts Ave. The Fourteenth and U Farmers Market is held at 14th & U Sts NW from 4pm to 8pm Wednesday, June to October.

DC Blues Festival

www.dcblues.org

Country blues, Chicago style and eastern seaboard sound: the Saturday of the Labor Day weekend attracts them all to this day-long party.

OCTOBER

High Heel Drag Race

Tuesday before Halloween showcases local drag queen derbies through Dupont Circle.

Marine Corps Marathon

www.marinemarathon.com

The 'People's Marathon,' fourth-largest in America, runs 26.2 miles from Arlington.

Taste of Georgetown

http://tasteofgeorgetown.com

Thirty of Georgetown's best get experimental, innovative – and affordable. Early to mid-October.

NOVEMBER

Election Day

Well, it's every four Novembers, and of course the election happens all over America. But nowhere else do you experience that mix of partisan passion, resigned cynicism, exuberant hope and tragic dejection as here, light at the end of the campaign tunnel for some, unattainable goal for others.

DECEMBER

National Christmas Tree & Menorah Lighting

The second Thursday of the month is the heart of the holiday season in the nation's capital, when the president rings in the holiday season and the festival of lights on the south lawn of the White House. Don't miss the Capitol's rival tree!

>ITINERARIES

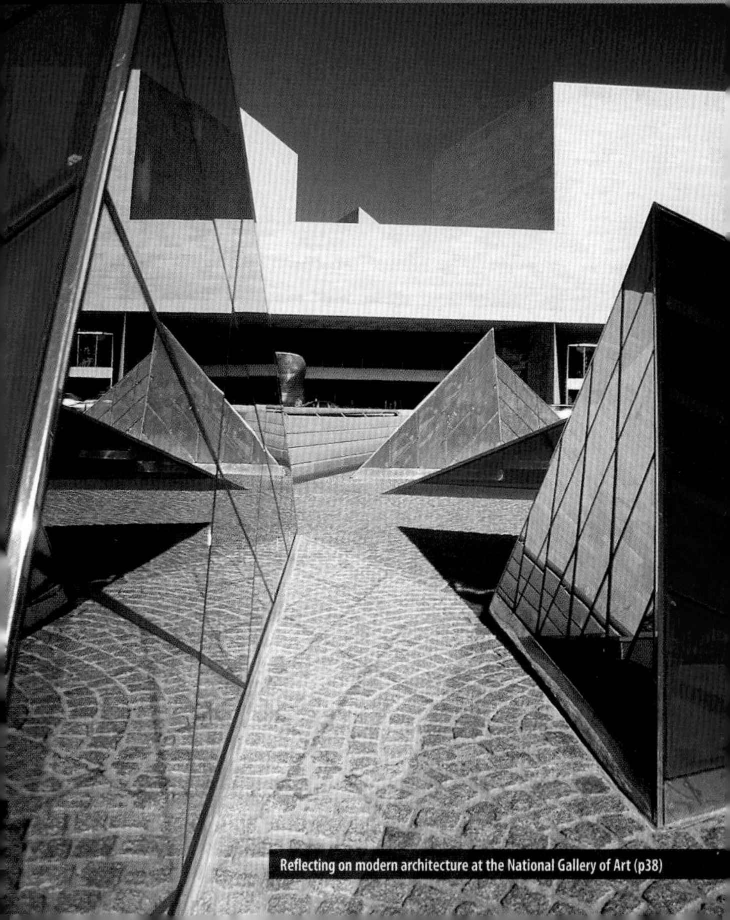

Reflecting on modern architecture at the National Gallery of Art (p38)

ITINERARIES

There's so much capital, so little time…and really, unless you live here, there's not enough time to enjoy all Washington, DC. Nonetheless, we've tried to pack together some top itineraries in a town that demands a fast pace and rewards you with sensory explosions and peeks into the American soul.

DAY ONE

Get yourself up early in the morning and head down to the National Mall (p34). You can't really do the whole thing in a day, so pick a museum, a monument and the Capitol (p43), and if you have time, grab lunch at the Mitsitam Café (p41). Once filled on some fine Native American fare, head up behind the Capitol again to pop into the Library of Congress (p46).

Go see the White House (p91) sparkle in the evening half-light. For dinner, pop up to Georgia Brown's (p93) and gorge on its excellent New South cuisine, and then ask yourself if you want to sleep or keep the night moving. If the latter, we'd recommend catching a cab to U St (p80) and picking a bar – we love Marvin (p86) – to give your DC day its perfect nightcap.

DAY TWO

Go to Pennsylvania Ave and see the documents that make America, well, America, in the National Archives (p38). But remember: this country is more than political pomp and circumstance. For the best exploration of her aesthetic side, walk to the Smithsonian American Art Museum, which connects the National Museum of American Art with the National Portrait Gallery (p56).

If you're looking for fun, we'd suggest heading east to the H St corridor, where you'll find the latest strip of interesting bars and restaurants to open in the capital. If the weather is cold, we'd recommend the coziness and bison burgers at Granville Moore's (p50), but if you'd like a little more space and the same good food, we'd vote for the Argonaut (p49). After you're done eating, there are plenty of bars along H and 14th where you can wild the night away.

Top Ascending the steps of the highest court in the land: the Supreme Court (p48) **Bottom** The axis of America: Lincoln Memorial (front; p37), Washington Monument (middle; p41) and the Capitol (back; p43), as seen from Arlington, VA

If you're not feeling too crazy, head from Downtown to Dupont Circle and take a walk amidst the café culture and foreign heads of states that make up this corner of town. For dinner, try Bistrot du Coin (p66), which serves the best steak frites in town.

DAY THREE

As the third day dawns, it's time to see some of the city outside of the main tourism hubs of the Mall and monuments. But we do ask that you see one more museum: the Historical Society of Washington, DC (p56), which will give you a good grounding in the living city you're about to explore.

Start your day with a walk along U St (p80) and pop into some of the shops, bars and restaurants opening on what seems like a weekly basis in this rapidly gentrifying part of town. Your lunch options are kind of limitless, but for a true DC diner experience, we need to get you into the Florida Avenue Grill (p85).

See a show at the Kennedy Center (p95) and then head to Columbia Heights for some dive-y fun at the Raven (p102) and dance-y follow up (well, if it's the weekend; otherwise sink another beer) at Wonderland (p103).

INTERNATIONAL ENCOUNTERS

This capital city may be known for her marble and monuments, but she's an immigrant entrepôt as well, and one of the most rewarding ways of seeing her is through international eyes.

But before we access Washington's immigrant enclaves, let's see her official international face. Starting in Dupont Circle, have a stroll up Em-

FORWARD PLANNING

Three weeks before you go Get reservations at Palena (see boxed text, p112) and see if you can join a White House tour (p91), although you'll want to look into the latter at least a month in advance.

One week before you go See what shows are playing on the listings pages of the *Washington City Paper* (www.washingtoncitypaper.com) and book tickets at the 9:30 Club (p87) and the Black Cat (p87), or plays at the Kennedy Center (p95).

One day before you go Do as Washingtonians do: read the *Washington Post* (www.washingtonpost.com) and check if there are any rallies, parades or protests that could enliven (or ruin) your getaway.

Patrons chowing down at Florida Avenue Grill (p85), DC's quintessential diner

bassy Row (p64) through the soil (well, near the soil) of dozens of foreign nations. Afterwards, turn around and grab a curry or some chicken rice at Malaysia Kopitiam (p67).

Mt Pleasant (p98) is the heart of Washington's enormous Salvadoran community, cut through by Mt Pleasant St, itself a small slice of Central America in the capital. There are all sorts of evocative images and sounds in the area, from blue-and-white flags to reggaeton pumping out of a basement walk-in, and good places to eat abound. While it isn't as 'authentic' as a true *pupuseria* (those little shacks where Salvadoran cheese and meat turnovers are sold), the folks behind the counter at Dos Gringos (p100), with its Anglo-Latin fusion fare, offer an accurate culinary digestion (heh) of this mixed-up 'hood. Finish the night back in Adams Morgan with some West African dancing and, if you're in the mood, debauchery at the Ghana Café (p113). Hope your legs aren't too sore in the morning.

>NEIGHBORHOODS

People having fun on the run in historic Georgetown (p70), DC's highest-end 'hood

NEIGHBORHOODS

It's too easy to observe that Washington is more than one city. What town isn't? But it's true that DC's component parts stand in stark relief when stacked next to each other. That's partly because even the most flag-loving patriot can't help but notice the dichotomy between the ideals embodied by the marbled federal capital and the dilapidation of surrounding projects.

But there are other divisions, more positive ones, besides the line between the regal capital and the rest. Because the city center is taken up by the National Mall, rather than a connecting commercial district, DC's districts have developed in relative isolation from each other, giving each 'hood its own unique stamp. As Washington has taken on the task of repopulating its inner core, the city has become more integrated, even as revitalized neighborhoods become more distinct from each other.

Today there's a marked shift in urban terrain between Georgetown's aristocracy, Dupont's gay upper crust, U St's clash of cultures, the Spanish-Amharic patois between Adams Morgan and Mount Pleasant and the hipster bars speckled between neighborhood hangouts on Georgia Ave. Residential Woodley Park, Cleveland Park and Tenleytown anchor DC's Upper Northwest, counterbalanced by the elegant row houses and pub-y scene of Capitol Hill. Further east, the experimental edge of DC's arts, music and foodie scene digs into rough and rising H St.

Chinatown – which is not that Chinese – runs west into Downtown, which tries to glitz itself up with new businesses every year or so. Further west, think tanks and international institutions – the business backbone of DC – make Foggy Bottom a bit bland, except for the glam White House. Across the Anacostia, Southeast DC struggles in the shadow of National Stadium, while on the far side of the Potomac, northern Virginia, home to Alexandria and Arlington, is a self-contained entity for families and youngsters who remain close but not too close to the capital's madcap swirl.

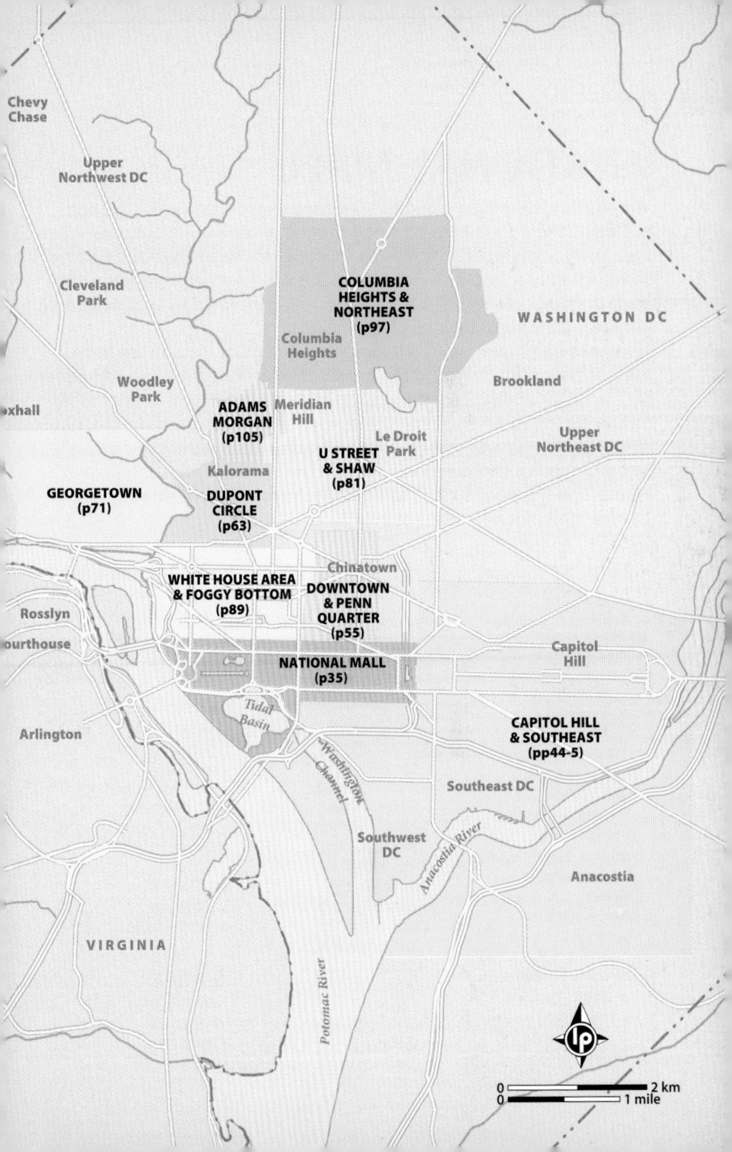

Chevy Chase
Upper Northwest DC
Cleveland Park
Woodley Park
COLUMBIA HEIGHTS & NORTHEAST (p97)
Columbia Heights
WASHINGTON DC
Brookland
ADAMS MORGAN (p105)
Meridian Hill
Le Droit Park
U STREET & SHAW (p81)
Upper Northeast DC
Kalorama
GEORGETOWN (p71)
DUPONT CIRCLE (p63)
Chinatown
WHITE HOUSE AREA & FOGGY BOTTOM (p89)
DOWNTOWN & PENN QUARTER (p55)
Rosslyn
Capitol Hill
NATIONAL MALL (p35)
Tidal Basin
Arlington
CAPITOL HILL & SOUTHEAST (pp44-5)
Washington Channel
Southeast DC
Southwest DC
Anacostia River
Anacostia
VIRGINIA
Potomac River
0 2 km
0 1 mile

>NATIONAL MALL

The Mall is often called 'America's front yard,' and that's a pretty good analogy – there's a reason it's stood the test of time. But let us posit a perhaps more apt allusion: the Mall as America's town green, in the original, New England sense of the word; the place where citizens gathered to learn the news of the day, debate the issues generated by that news and put ideas forward to their elected officials.

Instead of (or perhaps in addition to) the news of the day, we have museums for education and the American experience, enshrined. Instead of small public debate are the great rallies – from 'I Have a Dream' to 'A Million Moms' to 'Bring Them Home Now' – that have been the talking points of American conversation (and argument). But the town green was more than a serious spot. It was also where the village engaged in its leisure, and thousands of visitors take their time off here to wander the 1.9-mile green heart of the nation.

NATIONAL MALL

SEE

Arthur M Sackler Gallery 1 D3
Constitution Gardens 2 B2
Franklin Delano Roosevelt Memorial ...3 B4
Freer Gallery of Art 4 D3
Hirshhorn Museum 5 E3
Hirshhorn Sculpture Garden 6 E3
Korean War Veterans Memorial 7 B3
Lincoln Memorial 8 A3
National Air & Space Museum 9 E3
National Archives 10 E2
National Gallery of Art (East Building) ...11 F2
National Gallery of Art (West Building) ...12 E2
National Museum of African Art 13 E3
National Museum of American History 14 D2
National Museum of the American Indian 15 F3
National WWII Memorial 16 C3
Newseum 17 E2
Smithsonian Institution Building ...18 D3
Smithsonian's National Museum of Natural History 19 D2
Thomas Jefferson Memorial 20 C4
United States Botanic Garden 21 F3
United States Holocaust Memorial Museum ...22 D3
Vietnam Veterans Memorial 23 B2
Washington Monument 24 C3
Washington Monument Ticket Kiosk 25 C3

EAT

Cascade Café .... (see 11)
Mitsitam Café .... (see 15)
Pavilion Café 26 E2

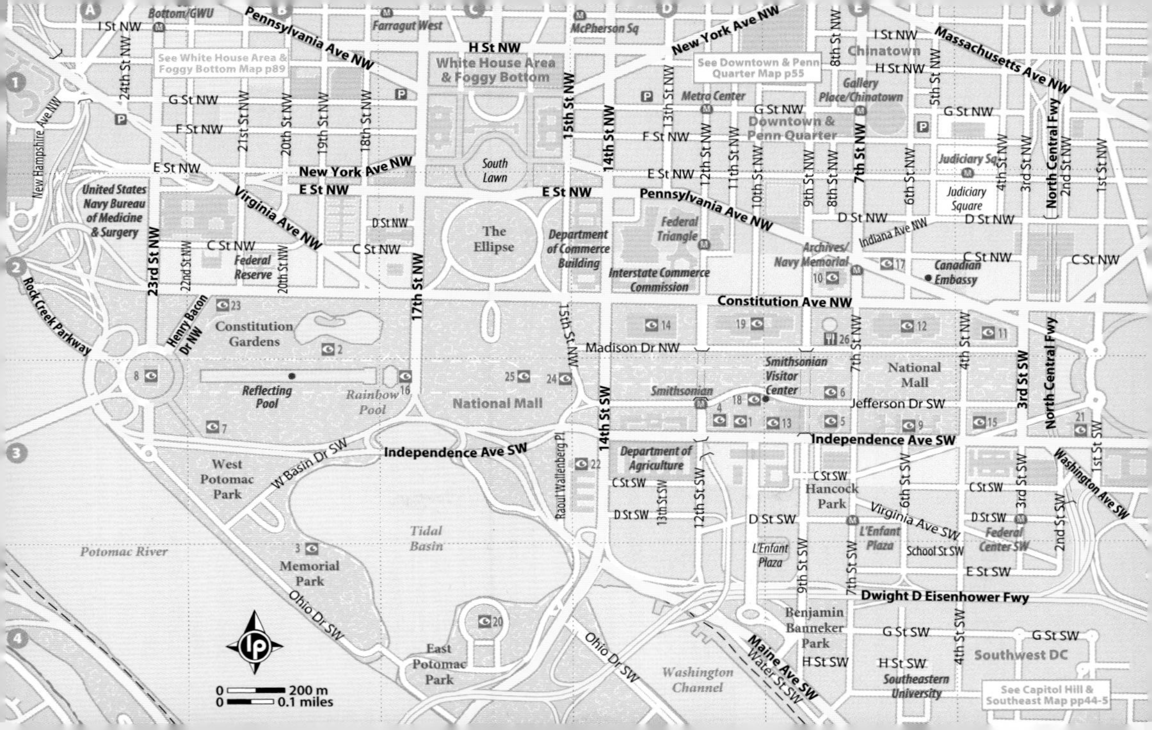

See White House Area & Foggy Bottom Map p89
See Downtown & Penn Quarter Map p55
See Capitol Hill & Southeast Map pp44-5
White House Area & Foggy Bottom
Chinatown
Downtown & Penn Quarter
Southwest DC
Pennsylvania Ave NW
New York Ave NW
Massachusetts Ave NW
Virginia Ave NW
Constitution Ave NW
Independence Ave SW
North Central Fwy
Dwight D Eisenhower Fwy
Rock Creek Parkway
Henry Bacon Dr NW
Madison Dr NW
Jefferson Dr SW
Indiana Ave NW
Virginia Ave SW
Washington Ave SW
Maine Ave SW
Water St SW
Ohio Dr SW
W Basin Dr SW
Raoul Wallenberg Pl
New Hampshire Ave NW
Bottom/GWU
Farragut West
McPherson Sq
Metro Center
Gallery Place/Chinatown
Judiciary Sq
Judiciary Square
Archives/Navy Memorial
Smithsonian
L'Enfant Plaza
Federal Center SW
South Lawn
The Ellipse
Department of Commerce Building
Federal Triangle
Interstate Commerce Commission
Canadian Embassy
United States Navy Bureau of Medicine & Surgery
Federal Reserve
Constitution Gardens
Reflecting Pool
Rainbow Pool
National Mall
Smithsonian Visitor Center
Department of Agriculture
Hancock Park
Benjamin Banneker Park
Southeastern University
West Potomac Park
Memorial Park
East Potomac Park
Tidal Basin
Potomac River
Washington Channel
0 200 m
0 0.1 miles

SEE

Unless otherwise noted, all museums have free admission and are open from 10am to 5:30pm daily. Although the National Archives and the Newseum are technically in Penn Quarter/Downtown, we've decided to include them here because by character and function they both belong to the Mall.

ARTHUR M SACKLER GALLERY/FREER GALLERY OF ART

☎ 202-633-1000; www.asia.si.edu; 1500 Independence Ave; M Smithsonian

These two collections combine to form the National Museum of Asian Art, and as a bonus, one of the most pleasant museums in which to while away a Washington afternoon. Japanese silk scrolls, Buddhas flashing Mona Lisa smiles and a treasure trove of Silk Road artifacts are complemented by an incongruous collection of paintings by the American master James Whistler.

CONSTITUTION GARDENS

www.nps.gov/coga; near Constitution Ave & 18th St SW; 24hr; M Smithsonian

A quiet collection of still ponds and paths, the gardens are a getaway on the Mall that feel remarkably hidden, sitting as they are in the middle of America's grand public thoroughfare. Look out for an island honoring the signatories to the Declaration of Independence.

FRANKLIN DELANO ROOSEVELT MEMORIAL

www.nps.gov/fdrm; Ohio Dr SW; 24hr; M Smithsonian

This innovative memorial honors both America's longest-serving president and the era he governed, via interconnected walkways that traverse a series of sometimes Dali-esque representations of the Depression, the New Deal and WWII.

HIRSHHORN MUSEUM & SCULPTURE GARDEN

http://hirshhorn.si.edu; near Independence Ave & 7th St SW; M Smithsonian

The Hirshhorn strikes a good balance between works by surrealists, pop artists and modernists such as Rodin, Calder and Warhol, and some suitably out-there conceptual, contemporary stuff. The museum also occasionally hosts evening concerts, improv shows etc. The sculpture garden is exactly that, a wonderful place for a surreal (if solo) or romantic (if coupled) stroll past masterpieces of modern art.

KOREAN WAR VETERANS MEMORIAL

www.nps.gov/kwvm; 8am-11:45pm; M Foggy Bottom

At the west end of the Mall, 19 steel soldiers wander through clumps of juniper past a wall bearing images of the 'Forgotten War' that assemble into a panorama of the Korean mountains. Best visited at night, when the sculpted patrol, representing all races and combat branches that served in the war, takes on a phantom cast.

LINCOLN MEMORIAL

www.nps.gov/linc; 23rd St SW; 24hr; M Foggy Bottom

In a city of icons, the inspiration for the back of the penny stands out in the crowd. It's the classicism evoked by the Greek temple design, or the way the memorial so perfectly anchors the Mall's west end, or maybe just the stony dignity of Lincoln's gaze and the power of his speeches engraved in the walls. Whatever; a visit here while gazing over the reflecting pool is a defining DC moment. Located at the west end of the Mall on 23rd St SW, between Constitution and Independence Aves.

NATIONAL AIR & SPACE MUSEUM

www.nasm.si.edu; Independence Ave & 4th St SW; M Smithsonian

The most popular Smithsonian museum holds the title because it's one of the best for kids, full of interactivity and fast things:

Able Abe keeping an eye on the capital from the Lincoln Memorial

Chuck Yeager's sound-barrier-breaking Bell X-1, Lindbergh's *Spirit of St Louis,* the Lunar Lander and the Wright Brothers' original airplane.

NATIONAL ARCHIVES

www.archives.com; 700 Pennsylvania Ave NW; M Archives-Navy Memorial

The archives, housed in an imposing neoclassical temple, are a must. There may be no greater electric surge between the American citizen and their country than the shock that occurs when reading the Constitution and the Declaration of Independence – the originals – under pale ambient light.

NATIONAL GALLERY OF ART

www.nga.gov; Constitution Ave & 4th St SW; M Smithsonian

An underground passage connects double galleries: the original, neoclassical west wing is primarily stuffed with European art from the Middle Ages to the early 20th century, with works by all the greats (including the continent's only da Vinci). The east wing, designed by IM Pei, is a little more abstract, a lot more conceptual.

NATIONAL MUSEUM OF AFRICAN ART

http://africa.si.edu; 950 Independence Ave SW; M Smithsonian

African aesthetics and creativity get good treatment here, with informative and often interactive displays that do a good job of mixing in modern and contemporary work with historical objets d'art from across the continent, which is rare for a museum on African art.

NATIONAL MUSEUM OF AMERICAN HISTORY

http://americanhistory.si.edu; Constitution Ave & 14th St NW; M Smithsonian, Federal Triangle

After undergoing a long series of renovations, this institution has accented itself with the daily bric-a-brac of the American experience – synagogue shawls, protest signs and cotton gins – plus an enormous display of the original Star-Spangled Banner and icons such as Dorothy's slippers and Kermit the Frog.

NATIONAL MUSEUM OF THE AMERICAN INDIAN

www.nmai.si.edu; Independence Ave & 4th St SW; M Smithsonian

Carved from golden sandstone and surrounded by simulated wetlands, this museum takes on a bit much and can feel thematically overwhelming, but the exhibitions are crucial for anyone with even a passing interest in indigenous peoples of the western hemisphere.

NATIONAL WWII MEMORIAL

www.wwiimemorial.com; 17th St SW; M Smithsonian

Almost dividing the Mall in half, this memorial consists of several components, including pavilions dedicated to the two main theaters of war (European and Pacific), a wall of gold stars and quotes from figures of the era. It's stirring and humbling, if just shy of being over-the-top. You'll find it between Constitution and Independence Aves.

NEWSEUM

☎ 888-639-7386; www.newseum.org; 555 Pennsylvania Ave; adult/child $20/10; M Archives-Navy Memorial

'The most interactive museum in the world' gives too much of the worst cable news has to offer: lots of flash, little substance. It's also a bit of sloppy self-love on the part of journalists – as if our egos weren't big enough. Still, it's great for the children, and the memorial to journos killed in pursuit of the truth, and exhibits on press freedoms and ethics make the price of admission worthwhile.

SMITHSONIAN INSTITUTION BUILDING

☎ 202-357-2700; www.si.edu; 1000 Jefferson Dr SW; 10am-5pm; M Smithsonian

Better known as 'the Castle,' this turreted, red-brick building evokes a Norman fortress, more elegant than imposing. The first Smithsonian building is the current HQ and visitor center for the institution.

SMITHSONIAN'S NATIONAL MUSEUM OF NATURAL HISTORY

www.mnh.si.edu; Constitution Ave & 10th St SW; M Smithsonian

Every kid's (and quite a few adults') favorite museum goes something like: dinosaurs, stuffed animals from every continent, an insect

Getting inside the media at Newseum

room, an elephant in the lobby, the Hope Diamond, Javanese shadow puppets and damn near everything else under the sun.

THOMAS JEFFERSON MEMORIAL

www.nps.gov/thje; Tidal Basin; 24hr; M Smithsonian

The words of the Declaration of Independence wrap around its author, who stands exposed to the elements in an open-air temple supported by Ionic columns. The nearby cherry trees lining the Potomac's tidal basin are especially beautiful in spring.

UNITED STATES BOTANIC GARDEN

www.usbg.gov; 245 1st St SW; M Federal Center

Over 26,000 species of plants huddle in seasonal displays and sticky humidity in the oldest continually operating botanical gardens in the country. The greenhouse effect (welcome here!) makes this the spot to rest after a cold winter Washington stroll.

UNITED STATES HOLOCAUST MEMORIAL MUSEUM

☎ 202-488-0400; www.ushmm.org; 100 Raoul Wallenberg Pl; M Smithsonian

Both a grim summation of human nature and a fierce confirmation of

A Washington Monument and Mall moment

basic goodness, this is a must-see. The main exhibit gives visitors the identity card of a single Holocaust victim, narrowing the scope of suffering to the individual level while paying thorough, overarching tribute to its powerful subject. Only a limited number of visitors are admitted to the memorial each day, so come early.

VIETNAM VETERANS MEMORIAL

www.nps.gov/vive; 24hr; M Foggy Bottom

A low-sloping black 'V' that cuts into the Mall and the American psyche, 'the Wall', inscribed with the names of some 58,000 casualties of the Vietnam War, is one of the most moving pieces of architecture in America.

WASHINGTON MONUMENT

www.nps.gov/wamo; 9am-5pm; M Smithsonian

Oldest joke in DC: 'So, what part of Washington is his monument modeled on?' Yeah, that's right, America has a bigger…obelisk than you. Peaking at 555ft (and 5in), the tallest building in the district took two phases of construction to complete; note the different hues of the stone. Tickets are free but must be reserved from the kiosk on 15th St between Madison and Jefferson Sts SW (8am to 4:30pm), or order in advance from www.nps.gov for $1.50.

EAT

Eating options are few and far between on the Mall, but these diamonds do shine even in the rough.

CASCADE CAFÉ *Café* $

202-712-7454; National Gallery of Art, Constitution Ave & 4th St SW; 11am-3pm Mon-Sat, to 4pm Sun; M Smithsonian

Located at the juncture of the wings of the National Gallery of Art, Cascade offers views of just that: a shimmering artificial waterfall that curtains off classical and modern art. It's one of the best coffee stops in any Washington museum. Food is of the soup and sandwich sort, and is available for picnic wrap-up if you'd like to eat outdoors.

MITSITAM CAFÉ

Native American $$

202-275-2110; National Museum of the American Indian, Independence Ave & 4th St SW; 10am-5:30pm; M Smithsonian

Without a doubt the best museum food on the Mall (if not in the country), the Mitsitam introduces visitors to the palette of regional American Indian cuisines, from the blue corn tortillas and slow-smoked barbecue of the Southwest to wild-rice-and-cranberry-stuffed turkey of the eastern woodlands.

PAVILION CAFÉ *Café* $

202-289-3361; www.pavilioncafe.com; Constitution Ave & 7th St SW; 10am-7pm Mon-Thu, to 9pm Fri & Sat, 11am-7pm Sun; M Smithsonian

Set amidst the rambling sylvan serenity of the sculpture garden at the National Gallery of Art, this pasta- and *panini*-style place makes for a green dream on spring days. From late May to October, free jazz concerts enrich the evening every Friday.

>CAPITOL HILL & SOUTHEAST

These 'hoods defiantly deny Washington's transient stereotype. While 'Capitol Hill' suggests uberpolitical atmosphere, this is also a neighborhood, where residents live in elegant row houses clumped into a community that revolves around the localvore/international arcade of Eastern Market. Hill pubs are local joints where the bouncer sports 'Skins caps; the feel of the place is more cozy borough than clandestine backroom. Just north is the H St corridor, an island of hip bars and restaurants that straddles one of DC's grittier edges.

Across the Anacostia is one of the oldest, blackest communities in town. Come here to see a community whose sense of identity is as strong as the go-go beat at an Oxon Hill house party, where locals respect, instead of ridicule, Marion Barry for earning a second chance – something that's as elusive as smoke on these hard-knock corners.

CAPITOL HILL & SOUTHEAST

SEE
- Anacostia Community Museum 1 G6
- Capitol 2 D2
- Capitol Grounds 3 D2
- Eastern Market 4 F3
- Folger Shakespeare Library & Theatre 5 E2
- Frederick Douglass National Historic Site ... 6 G6
- Library of Congress (Jefferson Building) ... 7 E2
- Nationals Stadium 8 E4
- Supreme Court 9 E2
- Union Station 10 E1

SHOP
- Remix 11 F3
- Woven History 12 F3

EAT
- Argonaut 13 G1
- Armand's Pizzeria 14 E1
- Fish Wharf 15 C3
- Granville Moore's 16 G1
- Jimmy T's 17 E2
- Market Lunch ..... (see 4)
- Montmarte 18 F3
- Sonoma Restaurant & Wine Bar 19 E3

DRINK
- Hawk & Dove 20 E3
- Phase 1 ..... 21 F3
- Red & Black 22 F1

PLAY
- Palace of Wonders 23 F1
- RFK Stadium 24 H2
- Rock & Roll Hotel 25 G1

Please see over for map

SEE

ANACOSTIA COMMUNITY MUSEUM

☎ 202-287-3306; www.si.edu/anacostia; 1901 Fort Pl SE; 10am-5pm; M Anacostia, then bus 94, W1, W2 or W6

This museum wears several hats: as community hall and museum for the surrounding black neighborhood of Anacostia and as a showpiece for rotating exhibits from the nomadic Smithsonian Museum of African American Culture (to have a home in 2010). The latter in particular are worth the trip here, but be aware that the museum can't really be walked to: you'll either need to hail a taxi, have your own wheels or take the bus.

CAPITOL & CAPITOL VISITOR CENTER

☎ 202-225-6827; www.aoc.gov; Visitor Center, 1st St NE; 9am-5pm; M Capitol South

The geographic center of the city is easily one of its most recognizable icons. That 285ft dome wraps around every memory you have of DC, even if you've never been here, because, like the New York skyline and the White House, it's an image owned by all Americans. In 2008 work was finally completed on a visitor center, which showcases the exhaustive background of a building that fairly sweats history, and also provides tours of the building – be on the lookout for statues of two famous residents per state, plus some of the most stunning baroque/neoclassical architecture in the nation.

SEEING CONGRESS IN ACTION

Watching Congress (which, if you didn't know, is based in the Capitol building) in session is easy. US citizens need to call their representative or senator's office (☎ 202-224-3121 for congressional directory); foreigners request passes from the House or Senate appointment desks on the 1st floor. You shouldn't be denied in either situation. Congressional committee hearings are actually more interesting (and substantive) if you care about what's being debated; check for a schedule, locations and to see if they're open to the public (they often are) at www.house.gov and www.senate.gov.

EASTERN MARKET

☎ 202-546-2698; www.easternmarket.net; 7th St & N Carolina Ave SE; 10am-6pm Tue-Fri, 8am-4pm Sat & Sun; M Eastern Market

The Capitol dome might win the word-image association game with visitors, but 'the Market' probably sweeps the title among locals when it comes to Capitol Hill. That's because Eastern Market makes the Hill a neighborhood as

A
B
C
D
1
2
3
4
5
6
Farragut West
McPherson Sq
H St NW
New York Ave NW
Downtown & Penn Quarter
Chinatown
Massachusetts Ave NW
Gallery Pl/Chinatown
Metro Center
White House
South Lawn
F St NW
13th St NW
9th St NW
See White House Area & Foggy Bottom Map p89
See Downtown & Penn Quarter Map p55
Judiciary Sq
3rd St NW
2nd St NW
New Jersey Ave NW
1st St NW
I St NW
G St NW
E St NW
Virginia Ave NW
Pennsylvania Ave NW
D St NW
C St NW
The Ellipse
15th St NW
Federal Triangle
Archives/Navy Memorial
Constitution Ave NW
17th St NW
Constitution Gardens
See National Mall Map p35
14th St SW
Madison Dr NW
National Mall
Smithsonian
Jefferson Dr SW
West Potomac Park
US Capitol
Independence Ave SW
W Basin Dr SW
US Postal Service
FAA Building
Hancock Park
Rayburn House Office Building
C St SW
D St SW
12th St SW
Federal Center SW
Virginia Ave SW
Tidal Basin
L'Enfant Plaza
School St SW
E St SW
Memorial Park
Dwight D Eisenhower Fwy
15
Maine Ave SW
7th St SW
G St SW
H St SW
4th St SW
1st St SW
I St SW
Water St SW
Lansburgh Park
K St SW
Half St SW
L St SW
14th St Bridge
East Potomac Park
Buckeye Dr SW
Ohio Dr SW
Washington Channel
6th St SW
Waterfront/SEU
M St SW
Delaware Ave SW
N St SW
Waterside Park
3rd St SW
O St SW
P St SW
East Potomac Park Golf Course
Southwest DC
Q St SW
B St
VIRGINIA
WASHINGTON DC
2nd Ave
5th Ave
Fort Lesley J McNair
R St SW
S St SW
2nd St SW
T St SW
Potomac River
C St
1st Ave
4th Ave
V St SW
George Washington Memorial Parkway
D St
Fort Lesley J McNair
Buzzard Point
Greenleaf Point
Ronald Reagan Washington National Airport
0 500 m
0 0.2 miles
Hains Point

E
F
G
H
1
2
3
4
5
6
Union Station
Florida Ave NE
Benning Rd NE
Maryland Ave NE
I St NE
H St NE
G St NE
Morris Pl NE
F St NE
Acker St NE
E St NE
D St NE
D St NW
C St NE
Gales St NE
Emerald St NE
Oklahoma Ave NE
Stanton Park
Capitol Hill
Massachusetts Ave NE
Tennessee Ave NE
North Carolina Ave NE
Constitution Ave NE
A St NE
E Capitol St
Lincoln Park
Parking Area
Library of Congress (Adams Building)
A St SE
North Carolina Ave SE
Massachusetts Ave SE
Independence Ave SE
Seward Square
South Carolina Ave SE
C St SE
D St SE
E St SE
Folger Park
Eastern Market
Marion Park
Stadium/Armory
Stadium/Armory Parking Area
Garfield Park
F St SE
G St SE
H St SE
Potomac Ave
Congressional Cemetery
US Marine Corps Barracks
Pennsylvania Ave SE
Kentucky Ave SE
New Jersey Ave SE
Virginia Ave SE
I St SE
K St SE
L St SE
M St SE
Potomac Ave SE
Southeast Fwy
Navy Yard
Tingey St SE
N St SE
N Pl SE
O St SE
Isaac Hull Ave SE
Patterson Ave SE
Paulding St SE
Dahlgren Ave SE
Parsons Ave SE
Southeast DC
Water St SE
Anacostia River
Anacostia Park
Nicholson St SE
Naylor Rd SE
Anacostia Fwy
Fairlawn Ave SE
Minnesota Ave SE
Q St SE
R St SE
Ridge Pl SE
S St SE
T St SE
U St SE
W St SE
Wells Memorial Bridge
Robbins Rd SW
Howard Rd SE
Anacostia
Martin Luther King Jr Ave SE
Good Hope Rd SE
Morris Rd SE
Randle Circle
S Capitol St
Fort Pl SE
1st St NE
2nd St NE
3rd St NE
4th St NE
5th St NE
6th St NE
7th St NE
8th St NE
9th St NE
10th St NE
11th St NE
12th St NE
13th St NE
14th St NE
15th St NE
16th St NE
17th St NE
18th St NE
19th St NE
20th St NE
21st St NE
22nd St SE
26th St NE
1st St SE
2nd St SE
4th St SE
5th St SE
6th St SE
7th St SE
8th St SE
9th St SE
10th St SE
11th St SE
12th St SE
13th St SE
14th St SE
16th St SE
19th St SE
2nd Pl SE
3rd St SE
17th St SE
18th St SE
22nd St SE
25th St SE
27th St SE

opposed to…well, a hill. Packed with good food, crafts and every ethnicity in the area, this roofed bazaar is a must-visit on weekends.

FOLGER SHAKESPEARE LIBRARY & THEATRE

202-544-4600; www.folger.edu; 201 East Capitol St; admission free; 10am-4pm Mon-Sat, tours 11am; M Capitol South

Bard-o-philes will be all of a passion here, with the largest collection of old Billy's works in the world. Stroll through the Great Hall of Elizabethan artifacts, see a show in the reconstructed Elizabethan Theatre and peek at rare items via the multimedia Shakespeare Gallery. Or visit April 23, when the entire collection is open to the public.

FREDERICK DOUGLASS NATIONAL HISTORIC SITE

202-426-5961; www.nps.gov/frdo; 1411 W St SE; admission free; 9am-4pm Sep-May, to 5pm Jun-Aug; M Anacostia, then bus B2, B4, W2 or 90

The hilltop home of the escaped slave, abolitionist, man of letters and icon of American civil rights is maintained as a nice museum that overlooks, in a figurative and literal way, the city and neighborhood that represents his nation's highest hopes and harshest realities. Start your visit with the corny intro movie in the visitor center.

LIBRARY OF CONGRESS

202-707-5000; www.loc.gov; 1st St NE & E Capitol St; admission free; 10am-5pm Mon-Sat; M Capitol South

Other sites might be more iconic, but this is our favorite place to bring new visitors to DC. It's both the look of the building, with it neoclassical architecture and embellishments that mix the intellectual heritage of the Old World with the optimism of the New, and its scope: amassing all the world's knowledge into this, its largest library. Special exhibitions are often excellent, and multimedia kiosks provide the minutest details of the library's awe-inspiring collection.

NATIONALS STADIUM

202-675-6287; 1500 S Capitol St SE; admission free; M Navy Yard

Everyone, even skeptics of baseball's neighborhood-rejuvenating powers, at least hoped the home of the Washington Nationals, DC's Major League Baseball franchise, could serve as a cornerstone for regeneration in the tough Southeast. Unfortunately, while the skin surrounding the stadium is scrubbed, past that the 'hood is hard. Catch a game if you can; the Nats, playing dozens of home games a season, are a strong social glue amongst DC's transients and natives – even though they've sucked for a while.

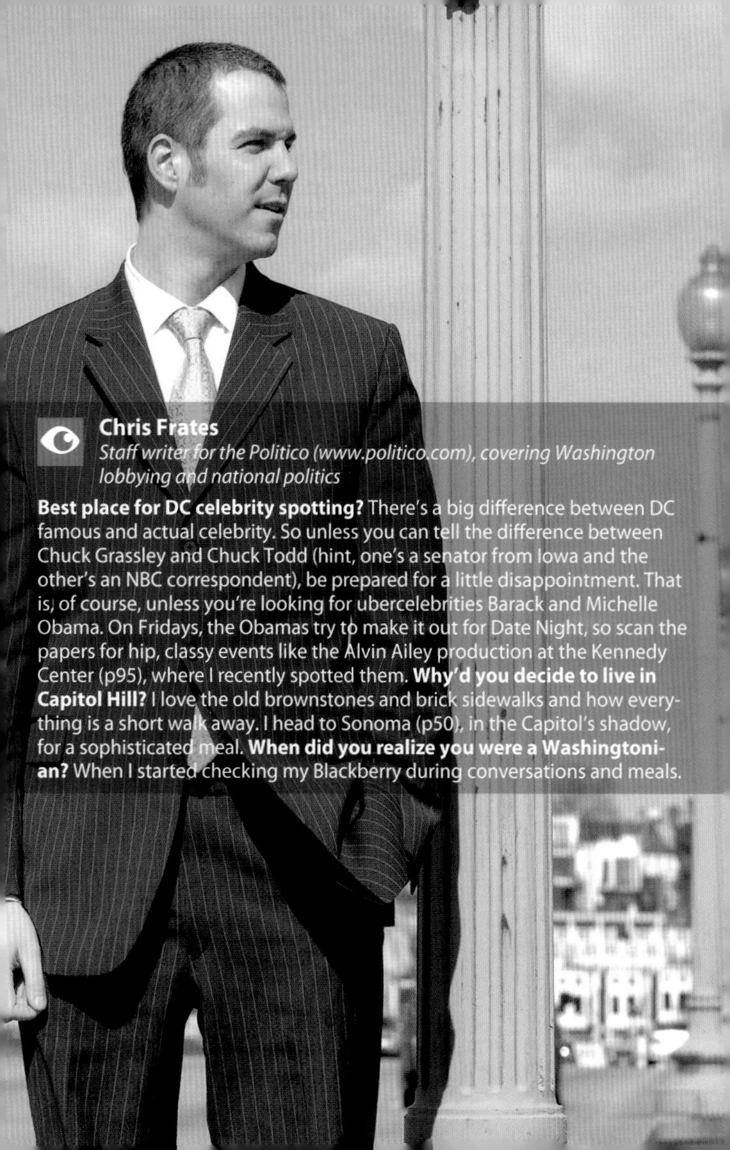

Chris Frates

Staff writer for the Politico (www.politico.com), covering Washington lobbying and national politics

Best place for DC celebrity spotting? There's a big difference between DC famous and actual celebrity. So unless you can tell the difference between Chuck Grassley and Chuck Todd (hint, one's a senator from Iowa and the other's an NBC correspondent), be prepared for a little disappointment. That is, of course, unless you're looking for ubercelebrities Barack and Michelle Obama. On Fridays, the Obamas try to make it out for Date Night, so scan the papers for hip, classy events like the Alvin Ailey production at the Kennedy Center (p95), where I recently spotted them. **Why'd you decide to live in Capitol Hill?** I love the old brownstones and brick sidewalks and how everything is a short walk away. I head to Sonoma (p50), in the Capitol's shadow, for a sophisticated meal. **When did you realize you were a Washingtonian?** When I started checking my Blackberry during conversations and meals.

SUPREME COURT

☎ 202-479-3030; www.supremecourt us.gov; 1 1st St NE; admission free; 9am-4:30pm Mon-Fri; M Capitol South

The highest court in the land is situated in (another) pseudo-Greek temple that you enter through 13,000lb bronze doors. Grounds are open to visitors, and you, along with the justices, can hear oral arguments from 10am Monday to Wednesday for two weeks every month from October to April; call or check the website to confirm and see what cases are being argued.

UNION STATION

☎ 202-289-1908; www.unionstationdc .com; 50 Massachusetts Ave NE; M Union Station

Even folks who use this 1907 beaux arts building as their work-commute station – ie those who should hate the sight of it – say they don't get tired of the Grand Concourse of Washington's main railhead. It's as impressive as a day in ancient Rome, which is what's depicted (specifically, the Baths of Diocletian) amidst the marble and gold filigree. B Smith's restaurant, in the east wing, was the old presidential waiting room, a pomp-y lounge for dignitaries.

Like a day in ancient Rome: the Grand Concourse at Union Station, a beaux arts beauty

SHOP

REMIX *Vintage*

☎ 202-547-0211; www.remixvintage.com; 645 Pennsylvania Ave SE; 11am-7pm Mon-Fri, to 8pm Sat, noon-6pm Sun; M Eastern Market

The owners of Remix have put a lot of effort into faithfully selecting iconic, or at least unique pieces for their discerning clientele, and while you pay a little more than at the average vintage shop, your style rewards are that much greater.

WOVEN HISTORY *Homewares*

☎ 202-543-1705; 311 7th St SE; 10am-6pm; M Eastern Market

It's like a Silk Road caravan got lost and pitched up near the Eastern Market. This lovely emporium is stuffed with crafts, carpets and tapestries from across Central Asia, Tibet and Mongolia, and unlike a lot of stores of this genre, feels more like an authentic tented bazaar than hippie hangout.

EAT

ARGONAUT *American* $$

☎ 202-216-5988; www.argonautdc.com; 1430 Maryland Ave NE; 5pm-2am Mon-Thu, 4pm-3am Fri, 1pm-3am Sat, 11am-2am Sun; M Union Station, then bus X8 or D8

You can get locally sourced organic goodness all around this town, but the setting is often some intimidating, chic spot straight from *The Matrix*. Not the 'Naut. It looks and feels like a corner spot where folks repair for a beer after work, and in truth, people still do so here. You should too, but don't miss the mouth-watering pumpkin ravioli or fries doused in Old Bay seasoning either.

ARMAND'S PIZZERIA *Pizza $*

☎ 202-547-6600; 226 Massachusetts Ave NE; 11am-9:30pm Mon-Fri, to 10pm Sat, 4-9pm Sun; M Union Station

The best pizza on the hill is served Chicago style (deep crust) and pleasantly greasy. It's almost next door to the right-wing Heritage Foundation, so depending on your politics, you can share some pie with Newt Gingrich or throw it at him.

FISH WHARF *Seafood* $

Waterfront, Washington Channel; 7:30am-8:30pm Sun-Thu, to 9pm Fri & Sat Sep-May, 7:30am-9:30pm Sun-Thu, to 10pm Fri & Sat Jun-Aug; M L'Enfant Plaza

In case you didn't know, Washington, DC is basically in Maryland, and Maryland does the best seafood in America. You get it fresh as hell – still flopping – here, where locals will kill, strip, shell, gut, fry, broil, whatever your fish, crabs, oysters etc in front of your eyes. Have a seat and a beer on the nearby benches and bliss out.

GRANVILLE MOORE'S *European* *$$*

☎ 202-347-5732; 1331 H St NW; 7am-10pm Mon-Sat, from 11am Sun; M Union Station, then bus X8 or D8

Dark and exuding the pure smells of beer, bison meat and mussels, this H St standout is the best of the many Belgian bistros that have been popping up around the city. The fireside setting is perfect on a winter's eve, and locals have been known to fall on their faces over the bison cheese-steak.

JIMMY T'S *American* *$*

☎ 202-546-3646; 501 E Capitol St; 7am-3pm Tue-Sun; M Eastern Market

Jimmy's is a neighborhood joint of the old school, where folks cram in to read the *Post*, have a burger or an omelette or some coffee and basically be themselves. If you're hungover on Sunday and in Cap Hill, this is the place to cure yourself.

MARKET LUNCH *Market* *$*

7th St & N Carolina Ave SE; 10am-6pm Tue-Fri, 8am-4pm Sat & Sun; M Eastern Market

You can eat well anywhere in Eastern Market, but this stall, across from Southern Maryland Seafoods, is our favorite. The food is obviously obtained locally and very fresh, with the fried oyster sandwich and lemonade leading the pack of our favorite DC weekend lunches.

MONTMARTE *European* *$$$*

☎ 202-544-1244; 327 7th St SE; 11:30am-2:30pm & 5:30-10pm Mon-Fri, 5:30-10pm Sat & Sun; M Eastern Market

Easily one of the top French spots in town, Montmarte is ensconced in a warm, neighborly location cluttered in a *maman's* dining room kinda way, complemented by great wines and some very fine steak, served bloody and yummy.

SONOMA RESTAURANT & WINE BAR *American* *$$$*

☎ 202-544-8088; www.sonomadc.com; 223 Pennsylvania Ave SE; 11:30am-2pm & 5:30-10pm Mon-Thu, 11:30am-2pm & 5:30-11pm Fri, 5:30-11pm Sat, 5-9pm Sun; M Eastern Market

Washington is a city that has embraced the wine bar genre with a vintner's passion, but there are a lot of mediocre executions of the genre about. Not Sonoma, where there's great meat, great grape and great pairings thanks to friendly, knowledgeable staff.

Cozy and inviting Granville Moore's, the place for Belgian bites

DRINK

HAWK & DOVE *Bar*

☎ 202-543-3300; 329 Pennsylvania Ave SE; to 2am; Ⓜ Capitol South

The quintessential hillie (congressional staff) hangout is dark, intimate and funner than you think; there's political shop talk, but also good beer, pool and, as the night wears on, the sort of fevered, across-the-aisle hook-ups DC is famous for.

PHASE 1 *Lesbian Bar*

☎ 202-544-6831; www.phase1dc.com; 525 8th St SE; 7pm-2am Wed, Thu & Sun, to 3am Fri & Sat; Ⓜ Eastern Market

'The Phase' claims to be the oldest lesbian bar in the country; it's certainly the best lesbian dive in DC, not that there's much competition for the crown. It's great, friendly fun by any measure, chockablock with jello wrestling, free pizza nights and an unpretentious but raucous enough atmosphere for ladies on the prowl.

RED & BLACK *Bar*

☎ 202-399-3201; www.redandblackbar.com; 1212 H St NE; 5pm-2am Mon-Fri, from 7pm Sat & Sun; Ⓜ Union Station, then bus X8

This dive-y New Orleans–style bar hosts some rockin' sets in its (bit too cramped) upstairs area. Downstairs things get congenially punk, and there's a nice beer garden in the back.

WORTH THE TRIP

Red-brick streets run under the flicker of cast-iron lamps and the steps of countless yuppies and suburbanites who love the twee charm of **Alexandria**. The northern Virginia 'burb (particularly its Old Town center) makes for a nice, studied jaunt in nostalgia-meets-the-mall.

The best reason to come here is to peruse the corridors of the **Torpedo Factory Art Center** (☎ 703-838-4565; www.torpedofactory.org; 105 N Union St; 10am-6pm Fri-Wed, to 9pm Thu; M King St), which answers the question: what do you do with a former munitions dump and arms factory? How about turn it into one of the best art spaces in the region? Three floors of artists' studios and free creativity are on offer in Old Town Alexandria, as well as the opportunity to buy paintings and sculptures directly from their creators.

Wealthy residents who often eschew going into DC have attracted lots of restaurants to this side of the Potomac; for lunch, we love to smell the air in **Cheesetique** (☎ 703-706-5300; www.cheesetique.com; 2411 Mt Vernon Ave; cheese & wine bar 11am-2:30pm & 5-9pm Tue-Thu, 11am-2:30pm & 5-10pm Fri & Sat, from noon Sun; M King St). Walking in feels like a whack – the impact of a sensory overload that anyone who's spent time in a good *fromagerie* will be familiar with. This is a cavern of wonders if wonders be cheese; there are few more civilized ways of spending an Alexandria evening than getting pleasantly drunk at the wine bar while sampling something new, stinky, runny and delicious.

Eamonn's Dublin Chipper (☎ 703-299-8384; www.eamonnsdublinchipper.com; 728 King St; 11:30am-10pm Mon-Wed, 11:30am-11pm Thu, 11:30am-midnight Fri, noon-midnight Sat, from noon Sun; M King St) bills itself as a 'Dublin' chipper. It upgrades fish and chips with authentic side touches like deep-fried Mars Bars, Milky Ways and Snickers and imported mushy peas. Plenty swear, and rightly so, by **Hank's Oyster Bar's** (☎ 703-739-4265; www.hanksdc.com; 1026 King St; 5:30-9:30pm Tue-Thu, 11:30am-10:30pm Fri, from 11am Sat, 11am-9:30pm Sun; M King St) original location in Dupont Circle, but the Old Town Alexandria setting just adds that extra whiff of nautical nostalgia and muddy Bay-watershed air. There's plenty of steak and such, but the main event, of course, is raw and on the half shell. If you've got a date (and a dinner jacket; dress codes are enforced), we recommend **Restaurant Eve** (☎ 703-706-0450; www.restauranteve.com; 110 South Pitt St; 11:30am-2:30pm & 5:30-10pm Mon-Fri, 5:30-10pm Sat; M King St) and its cod cheeks, pork belly, pan-fried sweetbreads and caviar, much of it locally sourced and all of it seasonally selected.

For a post dinner pick-me-up, stop by **Misha's Coffee Roaster** (☎ 703-548-4089; 102 S Patrick St; 6am-8pm Mon-Sat, from 6:30am Sun; M King St) and sip a lovely latte next to jars of beans from Indonesia and Ethiopia while banging out your play on your laptop (or procrastinating with the free wi-fi). If you need a beer, pop into **Tiffany Tavern** (☎ 703-739-4265; www.tiffanytavern.com; 1116 King St; 5pm-midnight Mon-Thu, to 2am Fri & Sat; M King St), which, besides serving pub grub and booze, is one of the best bluegrass venues around.

PLAY

PALACE OF WONDERS

Freak Show

☎ 202-398-7469; www.palaceofwonders.com; 1210 H St NE; 6pm-2am; M Union Station, then bus X8 or D8

Damn but DC needed this place: a permanent freak show. Seriously though, the Palace puts on fire eating, sword swallowing and flea circuses every week, performed by a cast of regulars and appreciated by a tattooed (or not) audience that sinks plenty of beers during intermission (and during shows too, come to think of it).

Tattooed lady center stage at Palace of Wonders

RFK STADIUM

Entertainment Center

☎ 202-547-9077; 2400 E Capitol St SE; M Stadium Armory

Thrown up way back in 1961, RFK is the oldest stadium in America built to accommodate football and baseball. Today it hosts neither (with the exception of some college football games); rather, it's the home of DC United, the local Major League Soccer franchise. RFK is a rickety old grumbler, known to physically shake when fans stomp their feet, but she's also well loved by anyone who grew up in the area – after the Redskins' last home game was played here, plenty of fans carted off the burgundy-and-gold stadium seats.

ROCK & ROLL HOTEL

Live Music

☎ 202-388-7625; www.rockandrollhoteldc.com; 1353 H St NE; 8pm-2am; M Union Station, then bus X8 or D8

The Hilton this hotel ain't, unless the Hilton went to hell and came back on a screaming motorcycle while wailing on guitars made of fire. OK, that's a tad hyperbolic, but this is a great, grotty spot to catch rockin' live sets. Don't let the name fool you: this hotel hosts some of the city's freshest hip-hop acts as well.

>DOWNTOWN & PENN QUARTER

For years, DC didn't have much of a Downtown, and we'd argue it's still deficient in these stakes. The uberdeveloped 'new' Downtown, also known as Penn Quarter, is less city center, more gussied-up transition space between the National Mall and Washington's neighborhoods. The office blocks, fast-food outlets and functional coffee shops that dot these concrete canyons keep the federal government running, but now, as in the past, they hold about nil interest to anyone not employed in them.

City fathers realized tourists often wandered these wilds with nothing to do, and have since gentrified the area into Downtown: anywhere, America. But DC is too idiosyncratic to be blanded up by Starbucks, and Penn Quarter sets itself off with great local restaurants, Chinatown – more like 'that string of Asian businesses between Hooters and Verizon Center' – and, of course, what we always do best in this town: museums. Some of our favorites are concentrated here, crowded off the National Mall but still within walking distance of Washington's monumental (pun intended) goodness.

DOWNTOWN & PENN QUARTER

SEE

- Chinatown Market 1 D4
- Friendship Arch 2 C4
- Historical Society of Washington, DC 3 C3
- International Spy Museum 4 C4
- National Public Radio 5 D3
- Smithsonian American Art Museum & National Portrait Gallery 6 C4

SHOP

- Apartment Zero 7 C5
- Coup de Foudre 8 B4
- Political Americana 9 A5

EAT

- Bistro d'Oc 10 B4
- Burma 11 D4
- Full Kee 12 D3
- Jaleo 13 C5
- Matchbox Pizza 14 C3
- Minibar at Café Atlantico 15 C5
- Zaytinya 16 C4

PLAY

- National Theatre 17 B5
- Verizon Center 18 D4

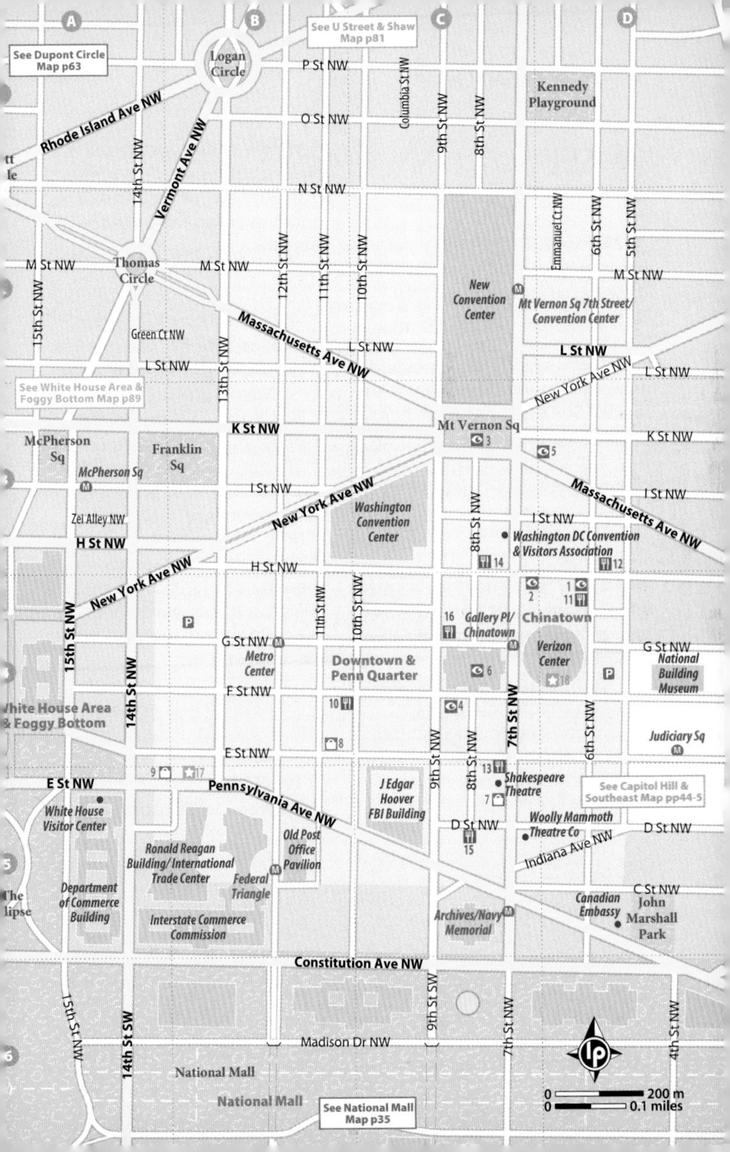

See Dupont Circle Map p63
See U Street & Shaw Map p81
Logan Circle
P St NW
O St NW
N St NW
M St NW
L St NW
K St NW
I St NW
H St NW
G St NW
F St NW
E St NW
D St NW
C St NW
Rhode Island Ave NW
Vermont Ave NW
Columbia St NW
Kennedy Playground
Thomas Circle
Massachusetts Ave NW
New York Ave NW
Pennsylvania Ave NW
Indiana Ave NW
Constitution Ave NW
Madison Dr NW
15th St NW
14th St NW
13th St NW
12th St NW
11th St NW
10th St NW
9th St NW
8th St NW
7th St NW
6th St NW
5th St NW
4th St NW
Emmanuel Ct NW
Green Ct NW
Zei Alley NW
New Convention Center
Mt Vernon Sq 7th Street/ Convention Center
Mt Vernon Sq
See White House Area & Foggy Bottom Map p89
McPherson Sq
Franklin Sq
Washington Convention Center
Washington DC Convention & Visitors Association
Gallery Pl/ Chinatown
Chinatown
Verizon Center
Metro Center
Downtown & Penn Quarter
National Building Museum
Judiciary Sq
White House Area & Foggy Bottom
J Edgar Hoover FBI Building
Shakespeare Theatre
See Capitol Hill & Southeast Map pp44-5
Woolly Mammoth Theatre Co
White House Visitor Center
Ronald Reagan Building/ International Trade Center
Old Post Office Pavilion
Federal Triangle
Department of Commerce Building
Interstate Commerce Commission
Archives/Navy Memorial
Canadian Embassy
John Marshall Park
15th St SW
14th St SW
9th St SW
National Mall
See National Mall Map p35
200 m
0.1 miles

SEE

HISTORICAL SOCIETY OF WASHINGTON, DC

☎ 202-785-2068; 800 Mt Vernon Sq; admission free; 10am-5pm Tue-Sun; M Mt Vernon Sq-Convention Center

Bless this DC-dedicated institution. Every other museum goes on about archaeology, airplanes and America, but what about our little capital? She explains herself here, in a wry, almost self-deprecating way; if you want to know her, please pop in.

INTERNATIONAL SPY MUSEUM

☎ 202-393-7798; www.spymuseum.org; 800 F St NW; adult/child $18/15; 10am-8pm Apr-Oct, to 6pm Nov-Mar; M Gallery Pl-Chinatown

This spy museum is great for kids, although anyone interested in espionage will enjoy the exhibits. That said, there's not much on the nitty-gritty of spy work (drudgery like code breaking, getting foreign assets to sell out their countries etc); you get the glamour here, with gadgets and doodads culled from real-life Q workshops.

NATIONAL PUBLIC RADIO

☎ 202-513-3232; www.npr.org; 635 Massachusetts Ave NW; admission free; tours 11am Thu; M Mt Vernon Sq 7th St-Convention Center

If, like us, you cannot complete the day without 'Morning Edition,' 'All Things Considered' and 'This American Life,' may we direct you to the wedgelike headquarters of NPR, the best thing to happen to radio since…nah, pretty much ever. Tours include strolls past the foreign and national desks and a peek into the organization's satellite control room.

SMITHSONIAN AMERICAN ART MUSEUM & NATIONAL PORTRAIT GALLERY

☎ 202-275-1500; www.americanart.si.edu; 9th & F St NW; admission

THAT'S IT?

The above phrase is often uttered by (brief) visitors to DC's dinky Chinatown, which you could pretty much trip over. Anchored on H and 7th St NW, this was once a major Asian entrepôt, but today most Washington-area Asians live in the Maryland/Virginia 'burbs. However small she may be, Chinatown is still entered through **Friendship Arch**, the largest single span arch in the world – thanks, sister city Beijing. This used to be an infamous boozer strip, now scrubbed and shiny thanks to the nearby Verizon Center (p61), but if you miss the old 'hood you can still buy a bottle of Mad Dog for under $3 at **Chinatown Market** (H & 6th St NW).

Espionage 101: International Spy Museum

free; 10am-8pm; M Gallery Pl-Chinatown

These two connected institutions must absolutely not be missed. Together, they constitute the largest collection of American art in the world, ranging from the fine to the modern to the folk, all displayed in an engaging space peppered with innovative special exhibitions. Head up to the top floor to walk through the magnificent former US Patent Office and annexes of more creative goodness.

SHOP

APARTMENT ZERO *Design*

☎ 202-628-4067; www.apartmentzero.com; 407 7th St NW; 11am-6pm Wed-Sat, noon-5pm Sun; M Archives-Navy Memorial

Try not to think of Apartment Zero as 'just' a design and homewares store. Framed by some of America's best art museums, it's more like a small special exhibition itself, displaying the cutting edge of American form and functionality – except the pieces here are for sale.

COUP DE FOUDRE *Clothing*

202-393-0878; www.coupdefoudrelingerie.com; 11th & E St NW; 11am-6pm Mon-Sat; M Metro Center

Local men dream of the day their girlfriends take them here and say, 'What should I get, honey?' The thing is, this isn't one of those unattainable male DC fantasies (like a 'Skins pennant). Women love Coup; the lingerie makes Vicky's Secret look gauche, and the mom-and-daughter owners have a passion for prettying up your bottom drawer.

POLITICAL AMERICANA *Gifts*

202-737-7730; www.politicalamericana.com; 1331 Pennsylvania Ave NW; 9am-8pm Mon-Sat, 10am-6pm Sun; M Metro Center

Well you can't leave without one Obama mug, right? Red-white-and-blue tat is ubiquitous in Washington, but this shop's collection of paraphernalia is a standout, from Truman posters to Mondale buttons to Barack Obama everything.

EAT

BISTRO D'OC *European* $$$

202-393-5444; www.bistrodoc.com; 518 10th St NW; 11:30am-2:30pm & 5:30-10pm Mon-Thu, to 11pm Fri & Sat, 11:30am-8:30pm Sun; M Metro Center

D'Oc is widely acknowledged as Washington's best place to impress with old-school French cuisine. It's supremely cozy, more Languedoc basement than lobbyist banter-bar. Think rich cassoulet and heavenly cheese plates, then stop thinking and order them.

BURMA *Asian* $

202-638-1280; 740 6th St NW; 11am-3pm & 6-10pm Mon-Fri, 6-10pm Sat & Sun; M Gallery Pl-Chinatown

If you haven't had Burmese food (hell, even if you have), get ye to this walkup and order some *ohn no kauk swe*, a coconut milk chicken soup that drives off winter chills with its amassed armies of delicious-ness. Dishes are oily and hot – but not overly so – and the setting is serene compared with the usual Chinatown chophouse.

FULL KEE *Asian* $

202-371-2233; 509 H St NW; 11:30am-2:30pm & 5:30pm-10:30pm Mon-Thu, to 11pm Fri & Sat; M Gallery Pl-Chinatown

This is an old-school Chinese cafeteria that you've surely eaten in before, except you haven't – the duck is divine, the sweet-and-sour soup an exemplar of the genre, and the atmosphere as barren as the moon. Don't complain, and pass the mambo sauce (DC's almost citrus-y version of sweet and sour).

Full Kee restaurant: you won't even notice the zero atmosphere when you tuck into the duck

JALEO *European* $$

☎ 202-628-7949; www.jaleo.com; 480 7th St NW; 🕒 11:30am-10pm Mon-Thu, to 11pm Fri, 5-11pm Sat, 10am-2:30pm Sun; Ⓜ Archives-Navy Memorial

One of DC's first tapas bars is still one of its best, ensconced in a Mediterranean mosaic that explodes with Andalucian pastiche. Sit down and suss out that sangria. The anchovies grilled in olive oil decidedly make the world go round.

MATCHBOX PIZZA *Pizza* $$

☎ 202-289-4441; www.matchboxdc.com; 713 H St NW; 🕒 11am-10:30pm Mon-Thu, to 1am Fri & Sat, to 10pm Sun; Ⓜ Gallery Pl-Chinatown

The pizza here rocketed into the DC gastronomic universe with a vengeance, and you can't come here now without finding a restaurant packed with the curious and the satisfied. What's so good about it? Fresh ingredients, a crust baked by angels and more fresh ingredients.

MINIBAR AT CAFÉ ATLANTICO *Modern* $$$

☎ 202-393-0812; www.cafeatlantico.com; 405 8th St NW; 🕒 seatings 6pm & 8:30pm Tue-Sat; Ⓜ Archives-Navy Memorial

Atlantico's minibar is foodie nirvana, where the curious get wowed by animal bits spun into cotton candy and cocktails frothed into clouds and all the conceptualization of food that says we, as a society, have a lot of time on our hands. The tasting menu, entirely determined by the chef, is often delicious, and at least original. Reservations a must.

ZAYTINYA *European* $$

202-333-4710; www.zaytinya.com; 701 9th St NW; 7:30am-1am Mon-Fri, from 8:30am Sat & Sun; M Gallery Pl-Chinatown

Somewhere between Lebanon, Greece and the high stone walls of contemporary design emerges Zaytinya, a popular power-lunch spot that happens to serve immaculate meze (like tapas) brought to you by immaculate waiters dressed like immaculate ninjas.

PLAY

NATIONAL THEATRE

Performing Arts

202-628-6161; www.nationaltheatre.org; 1321 Pennsylvania Ave NW; M Federal Triangle

Washington's oldest continually operating theater has been staging shows since 1835; we're not

A bird's-eye view of the hallowed halls of Zaytinya

FREE FUN!

Besides the Smithsonian, of course, there's plenty of fun to be had for gratis in the District. Some of our favorite free activities in town:

> Day-tripping in Malcom X Park (p106)
> Window browsing along M St, Georgetown (p70)
> Watching Congress (p43)
> Seeing – and smelling – Eastern Market (p43) on Sunday morning
> An Embassy Row (p64) amble
> Summer jazz in the Sculpture Garden (p36), 7th St & Constitution Ave NW, around 6pm

sure what the lineup was like then, but today this is the spot to catch big-name main-stage productions along the lines of *Les Miserables.* It's a big and beautiful venue and very few seats, with the exception of some nosebleeds, disappoint. Come on Monday nights at 6pm and 7:30pm for free performances.

VERIZON CENTER

Entertainment Center

☎ 202-661-5000; www.verizoncenter.com; 601 F St NW; Ⓜ Gallery Pl-Chinatown

Home of the Washington Capitals (NHL) and Washington Wizards (NBA), the Verizon Center also hosts lots of DC's biggest headliner concerts.

>DUPONT CIRCLE

For decades Dupont served as the midrange heart of all those activities that make city life so special. Here you found flash new restaurants, hip bars, café society and folk-singer-esque bookshops, a place where those possessed of creativity and common means could convene. The embassies in their stately mansions lined the Row, and the out-and-about pulse of DC's gay and lesbian community topped the whole shebang off. If you needed to live life as an urbanite, tasting off the tapas menu of cosmopolitan living, you generally did so here.

All of the above is still here – it's just no longer restricted to Dupont. But by no means does this allow you to pass up the Circle. On a summer night, when that unmistakable DC golden haze hovers over the alleys, it doesn't illuminate any other part of town more than the outdoor, artistic and accepting facade of one of Washington's great neighborhoods.

DUPONT CIRCLE

SEE

Embassy Row 1 C2
Phillips Collection 2 C2
Textile Museum 3 B1

SHOP

Green & Blue 4 D3
Lambda Rising 5 D2
Tabletop 6 C2

EAT

Annie's Paramount Steakhouse 7 E2
Bistrot du Coin 8 C1
Kramerbooks & Afterwords Café 9 D2
Malaysia Kopitiam 10 D4
Tabard Inn 11 E3

DRINK

Big Hunt 12 D3
Brickskeller 13 C2
Lucky Bar 14 D4

PLAY

18th Street Lounge 15 D4
Apex 16 C3
Cobalt 17 E2
Omega 18 C3

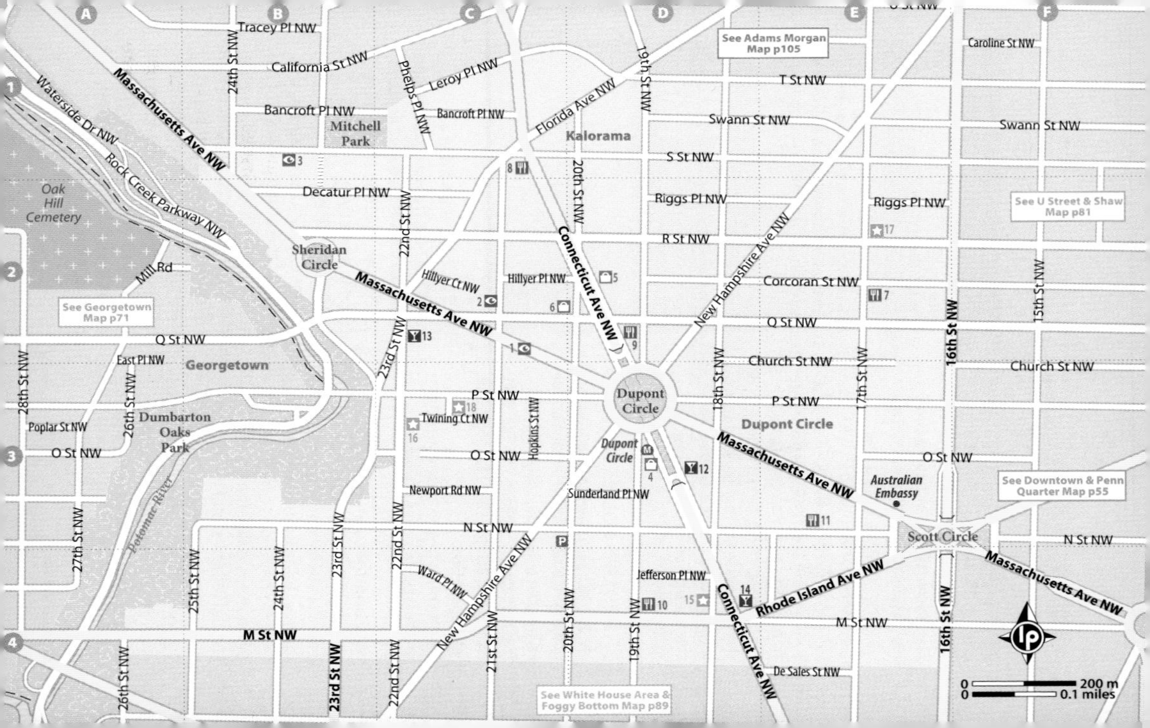

See Adams Morgan Map p105
See U Street & Shaw Map p81
See Georgetown Map p71
See Downtown & Penn Quarter Map p55
See White House Area & Foggy Bottom Map p89
Tracey Pl NW
California St NW
Bancroft Pl NW
Mitchell Park
Phelps Pl NW
Leroy Pl NW
Florida Ave NW
Kalorama
19th St NW
Caroline St NW
T St NW
Swann St NW
S St NW
Riggs Pl NW
R St NW
Corcoran St NW
Q St NW
Church St NW
P St NW
O St NW
N St NW
M St NW
De Sales St NW
Jefferson Pl NW
Sunderland Pl NW
Newport Rd NW
Hopkins St NW
Twining Ct NW
Hillyer Ct NW
Hillyer Pl NW
Ward Pl NW
Decatur Pl NW
Massachusetts Ave NW
Connecticut Ave NW
New Hampshire Ave NW
Rhode Island Ave NW
Waterside Dr NW
Rock Creek Parkway NW
Oak Hill Cemetery
Mill Rd
Sheridan Circle
Dupont Circle
Scott Circle
Australian Embassy
Georgetown
East Pl NW
Poplar St NW
Dumbarton Oaks Park
Potomac River
15th St NW
16th St NW
17th St NW
18th St NW
20th St NW
21st St NW
22nd St NW
23rd St NW
24th St NW
25th St NW
26th St NW
27th St NW
28th St NW
200 m
0.1 miles

SEE

EMBASSY ROW

Massachusetts Ave; M Dupont Circle

How quickly can you leave the country? It takes about five minutes; just stroll north along Mass Ave from Dupont Circle (the traffic circle the neighborhood is named for) and you pass roughly 50 embassies housed in mansions that range from the elegant to the imposing to the out there, plus the foreign soil they technically rest on.

PHILLIPS COLLECTION

☎ 202-387-2151; www.phillipscollection.org; 1600 21st St NW; admission Tue-Fri free, Sat & Sun $10, special exhibit fees may apply; 10am-5pm Tue, Wed, Fri & Sat, to 8:30pm Thu, 11am-6pm Sun; M Dupont Circle

Don't think of the oldest modern art museum in the country as a gallery; it's more like a great house, immaculately designed and dappled with some of the best creativity you'll ever see for free. Van Gogh, Rothko and O'Keefe paintings grace the permanent collection, while special exhibits pull in conceptual talent such as Christo. Over 22,000 sq ft of a 2006-added wing is underground, out of respect for the surrounding Georgian neighborhood.

THE 44TH PRESIDENT

The nation's capital is majority African American and staunchly liberal, which may be why it's embraced Barack Obama with near-religious fervor. Barack has returned the love, playing pick-up basketball and meeting-and-greeting in DC 'hoods ne'er graced by executive smile. Some whisper the 44th President of the United States may become something unique: a Washingtonian. Make sure you pick up Obamania souvenirs when you visit; we like rhinestone-studded Obama caps at **Skynear & Co** (p109), Picasso-esque portraits in **Eastern Market** (p43), children's books on Obama's bio in **Kramerbooks** (p67) and, of course, airbrushed tees and hoodies displaying the first family, which can be purchased on every block.

TEXTILE MUSEUM

☎ 202-667-0441; www.textilemuseum.org; 2320 S St NW; suggested donation $5; 10am-5pm Mon-Sat, from 1pm Sun; M Dupont Circle

A DC gem that even long-time residents barely know about, this is one of the best museums of its kind in the world. Started, like so many great things, by an eccentric collector (George Hewitt Myer), this little upstart culls cloth from around the world, in the form of tapestries, carpets etc, into a space as visually arresting as a small Smithsonian.

SHOP

GREEN & BLUE *Clothing*

☎ 202-223-6644; 1350 Connecticut Ave NW; 10am-8pm Mon-Fri, 11am-7pm Sat, noon-6pm Sun; M Dupont Circle

The boutique may be named for soothing colors, but its cool tones aren't just swathes of the palette: there are plenty of smart blouses, clutches and assorted accessories here that run the rainbow in terms of presentation, and all suggest style.

LAMBDA RISING *Books*

☎ 202-462-6969; 1625 Connecticut Ave NW; 10am-10pm Sun-Thu, to midnight Fri & Sat; M Dupont Circle

If Dupont Circle is the heart of gay DC, Lambda is its head (which would put the head in the heart…whatever). It carries an excellent collection of gay and lesbian books and videos, and is a good pulse point if you want to feel what's up in the gay and lesbian community.

TABLETOP *Design*

☎ 202-387-7117; www.tabletopdc.com; 1608 20th St NW; noon-8pm Mon-Sat, to 6pm Sun; M Dupont Circle

Also known as the best little design store in Dupont, Tabletop is evidence that DC is a lot more chic than some give it credit for. It's kooky candles, postmodern purses

A DC treasure unknown even to locals: the Textile Museum

What better combination than brunch and books? Kramerbooks & Afterwords Café

and postindustrial homewares; taken together, your living space will be pampered.

EAT

ANNIE'S PARAMOUNT STEAKHOUSE

Steakhouse $$

☎ 202-322-0395; 1609 17th St NW; 11:30am-11:30pm Mon-Thu, 24hr Fri-Sun; M Dupont Circle

We have to admit: Annie's has gone a little downhill. It's just not as…warm as it once was. But the clientele of Washington's favorite gay steakhouse is loyal, and still stuffs the walls for weekend breakfast and brunch. It's an endearingly social, sometimes socially awkward scene, as well-heeled Dupont families eat eggs next to two guys who realize they might have hooked up at Apex (p68).

BISTROT DU COIN

European $$

☎ 202-234-6969; www.bistrotducoin.com; 1738 Connecticut Ave NW; 11:30am-11pm Sun-Wed, to 1am Thu-Sat; M Dupont Circle

The Bistrot is both exemplar and exaggeration of a working-man Parisian joint, serving groaningly delicious plates of steak frites, mussels and a lovely *lapin* (rabbit) stew. Often packed with Europeans who know where to get the good stuff.

KRAMERBOOKS & AFTERWORDS CAFÉ

American $$

☎ 202-387-1462; www.kramers.com; 1738 Connecticut Ave NW; 7:30am-1am Sun-Thu, 24hr Fri & Sat; M Dupont Circle

Generations of DC intelligentsia swear by this combination awesome bookstore and awesome-squared brunch spot (pecan-crusted catfish with hollandaise, anyone?). Browsing the stacks before stuffing your guts is a terrific way to spend a DC weekend.

MALAYSIA KOPITIAM

Asian $$

☎ 202-833-6232; 1827 M St NW; 11:30am-10pm Mon-Thu, to 11pm Fri & Sat, noon-10pm Sun; M Farragut North or Dupont Circle

If you're familiar with Malaysian food, this is as close as you'll get to a Penang street stall in DC. If you're not, may we introduce you to: *laksa*, bowls of noodle soup cut with coconut milk and pillow-y chunks of chicken, spiced dried fish, and anything cooked in banana leaves. It's next door to Camelot, DC's most (in)famous stripper bar.

TABARD INN

American $$

☎ 202-331-8528; 1739 N St NW; breakfast 7-10am Mon-Fri, 8-9:45am Sat, to 9:15am Sun, brunch & lunch 11:30am-2:30pm Mon-Fri, from 11am Sat, from 10:30am Sun, dinner 6-9:30pm Sun-Thu, to 10pm Fri & Sat; M Dupont Circle

In a city that loves its brunches, it's unfair Dupont gets two standouts of the genre (see Kramerbooks, left), but the gods put the Tabard here and we mortals must contend. Dinners are great, but it's the deceptively normal brunch menu, with poached eggs, pecan waffles etc, that stands out. The ingredients (including oysters caught specifically for the inn) are just so good it's like brunch enlightened.

DRINK

BIG HUNT *Lounge*

☎ 202-785-2333; 1345 Connecticut Ave NW; noon-2am Sun-Thu, to 3am Fri & Sat; M Dupont Circle

If you just said the name of this bar and smiled a little inner smile (or turned red), well, that's kinda the point. The irreverence is carried on inside via two floors of general tomfoolery, including one of the city's better rooftop patios and some of the best pool tables.

BRICKSKELLER

Beerstravaganza

☎ 202-293-1885; 1523 22nd St NW; 11:30-2am Wed-Fri, from 5pm Sat-Tue; M Dupont Circle

The ambience is cavernous yet cozy and the staff friendly in the

THE CAPITAL PLAYLIST

Tracks by Washington artists and where to play 'em:

> 'Waiting Room,' by Fugazi – H St
> 'Mood Indigo,' by Duke Ellington – Logan Circle to Shaw
> 'The District Sleeps Tonight,' by The Postal Service – 16th St NW
> 'Bustin' Loose,' by Chuck Jones – Georgia Ave
> '1 Thing,' by Amerie – Adams Morgan
> 'Banned in DC,' by Bad Brains – Columbia Heights
> 'Overnight Scenario,' by Rare Essence – Southeast
> 'Sentimental Mood,' by Ella Fitzgerald – National Mall

way of aficionados sharing a passion – that being a passion for one of the largest beer menus in the world. The menu is amazing: booze that runs from Sierra Nevada to Sierra Leone (probably) and everywhere in between. Aim for a corner seat in the 'Skeller's cellar.

LUCKY BAR *Bar*

☎ 202-331-3733; 1221 Connecticut Ave NW; ⌚ noon-2am; Ⓜ Dupont Circle

Lucky's interior is nothing special, just your standard double-decker dark wood and cozy chairs. It's the crowd that sets this bar apart, which is an amalgamation of capital subcultures including politicos, Dupont gay couples, club kids needing a break from thumpa-thumpa and the occasional tourist, everyone enjoying eveyone else over a happy booze-fueled drone.

PLAY

18TH STREET LOUNGE *Club*

☎ 202-466-3922; 1212 18th St NW; ⌚ 9:30pm-2am Tue & Wed, from 5:30pm Thu, 5:30pm-3am Fri, from 9:30pm Sat; Ⓜ Dupont Circle

No signs here – just look for the lines stretching round the block. The Lounge, located in Teddy Roosevelt's old digs, is several floors of upholstered hip and hip-hop album cover, inhabited by guys and gals suitably attired for attracting attention (and if lucky, action). Music is several cuts above pop 40 pap, but attitude remains relatively down to earth, if still pretty posh.

APEX *Gay Club*

☎ 202-296-0605; 1415 22nd St NW; ⌚ 9pm-2am Tue & Thu-Sun; Ⓜ Dupont Circle

By Apex, we mean the heights of Washington's gay clubbing. The interior is predictable: lots of boys, lots of beats and fewer and fewer shirts as the evening wears on. On good nights everyone is dancing too much to care much about anything, but on bad ones it gets cruise-y like Carnival, with way too many early 20-somethings leading round men twice their age.

COBALT *Gay Club*

202-462-6569; 1639 R St NW; 5pm-2am; M Dupont Circle

Between Apex and Omega – conceptually, that is – lays Cobalt, a lounge-y bar on one floor, clubtastic gay fun on the other. There are nights when the dance floor seems as popular with straight ladies as gay guys, to the clear chagrin of the latter.

OMEGA *Gay Bar*

202-223-4917; 2122 P St NW; 4pm-2am Mon-Fri, from 8pm Sat, from 7pm Sun; M Dupont Circle

Apex and Omega, by name and by nature, are at opposite ends of DC's gay scene. Where the former is unsa-unsa all the way, the latter is a two-story bar where everyone knows your name and the clientele is likely as not white – or black; politically connected or never been on the Hill; and, to an often bear-ish man, friendly. Alright, it's not all congenial gay camaraderie: on Wednesday nights shirtless men drink for free from 10pm to 11pm.

>GEORGETOWN

If you have a thing for fine Federal architecture, lots of shopping, cobblestone streets, outdoor café culture and river views – all sprinkled with hard-studying and harder-partying college students – you, my friend, are in patrician paradise. Georgetown has always been Washington's house on the hill, and it comes with all the requisite high-end shopping, dining and nightlife such luxury affords.

Haters say Georgetown is an elitist institution of a district, and it's true there are lots of tricked-out SUVs driven by guys in J Crew khakis and with J Crew haircuts on these streets. But if we anthropomorphize the area, it's also an Indian student of international relations who's part-timing a stint at the World Bank, a classics professor who volunteers in heritage houses on weekends and a designer seeking an upscale market and less competition than NYC. If this is DC's highest-end 'hood, she's as smart as she is attractive, and not half as haughty as she could be.

GEORGETOWN

SEE

C&O Canal Towpath	1	B3
C&O Canal Visitor Center	2	D3
C&O Canal	3	B3
Capital Crescent Trail (Start)	4	C3
Dumbarton Oaks	5	D2
Exorcist Steps	6	C3
Georgetown University	7	C3
Georgetown Waterfront Park	8	E4
Old Stone House	9	D3

SHOP

Big Planet Comics	10	D3
Cady's Alley	11	C3
Lantern	12	D2
Proper Topper	13	D3
Relish	14	C3
Tugooh Toys	15	D3

EAT

1789	16	C3
Baked & Wired	17	D4
Café Milano	18	D3
Citronelle	19	E3
Hook	20	D3
Martin's Tavern	21	D3

DRINK

Mie N Yu	22	D3
Mr Smith's	23	D3
Tombs	(see 16)	

PLAY

Blues Alley	24	D3

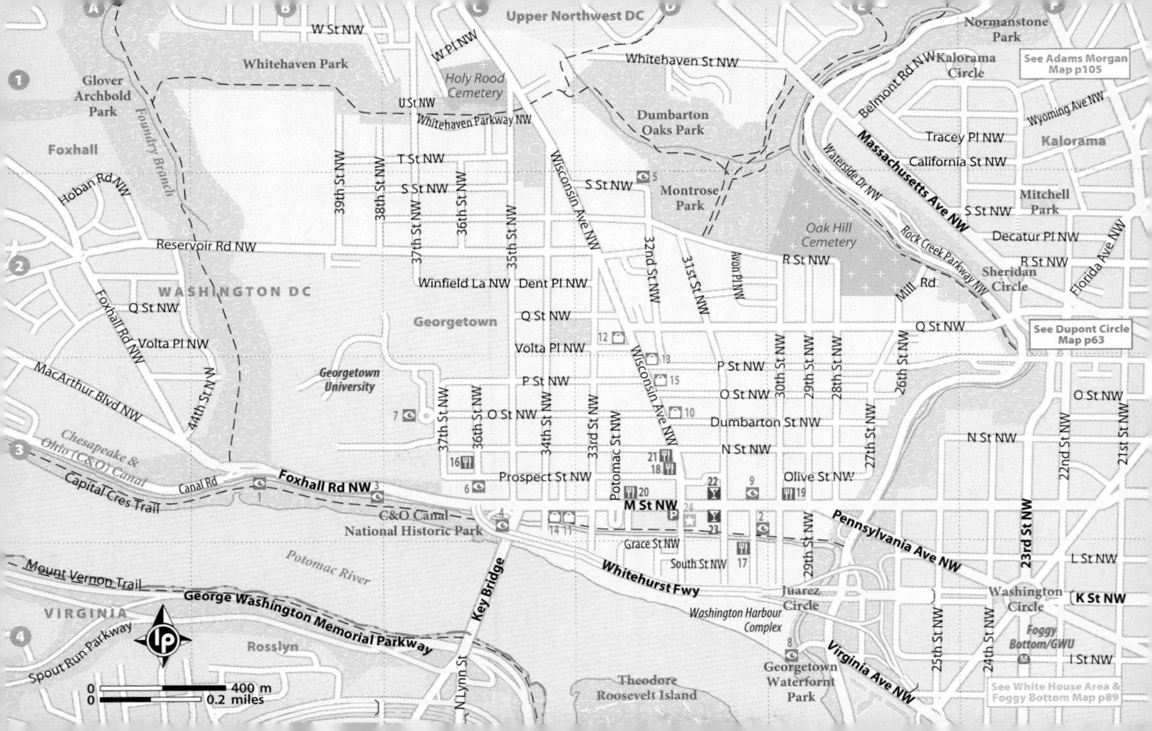
Upper Northwest DC
W St NW
W Pl NW
Whitehaven Park
Holy Rood Cemetery
Whitehaven St NW
Normanstone Park
Kalorama Circle
Belmont Rd NW
See Adams Morgan Map p105
Glover Archbold Park
Foundry Branch
U St NW
Whitehaven Parkway NW
Dumbarton Oaks Park
Wyoming Ave NW
Tracey Pl NW
Kalorama
California St NW
Foxhall
Hoban Rd NW
T St NW
S St NW
39th St NW
38th St NW
37th St NW
36th St NW
35th St NW
Wisconsin Ave NW
Montrose Park
Waterside Dr NW
Massachusetts Ave NW
Mitchell Park
Oak Hill Cemetery
Decatur Pl NW
Reservoir Rd NW
32nd St NW
31st St NW
Avon Pl NW
R St NW
Rock Creek Parkway NW
Sheridan Circle
Florida Ave NW
WASHINGTON DC
Winfield La NW
Dent Pl NW
Mill Rd
Q St NW
Foxhall Rd NW
Volta Pl NW
Georgetown
See Dupont Circle Map p63
P St NW
30th St NW
29th St NW
28th St NW
26th St NW
MacArthur Blvd NW
Georgetown University
O St NW
44th St NW
Dumbarton St NW
27th St NW
N St NW
22nd St NW
21st St NW
34th St NW
33rd St NW
Potomac St NW
Chesapeake & Ohio (C&O) Canal
Prospect St NW
Olive St NW
Canal Rd
Capital Cres Trail
M St NW
23rd St NW
C&O Canal National Historic Park
Pennsylvania Ave NW
Grace St NW
South St NW
L St NW
Potomac River
Whitehurst Fwy
Mount Vernon Trail
Key Bridge
Juarez Circle
Washington Circle
K St NW
George Washington Memorial Parkway
Washington Harbour Complex
VIRGINIA
Foggy Bottom/GWU
Spout Run Parkway
Rosslyn
Georgetown Waterfront Park
Virginia Ave NW
25th St NW
24th St NW
I St NW
N Lynn St
Theodore Roosevelt Island
400 m
0.2 miles
See White House Area & Foggy Bottom Map p89

SEE

There is no Metro station in Georgetown, but the DC Circulator bus ($1) connects the neighborhood to Foggy Bottom, Farragut North, Farragut West and Union Station.

C&O CANAL & TOWPATH

202-653-5190; www.nps.gov/choh; 1057 Thomas Jefferson St NW; 10am-4pm

The C&O Canal runs from here to West Virginia, and once brought goods and passengers from the capital to the then-beginning of the American West. Today the canal's towpath (boats were once hauled by horse) marks the start of a fabulous hiking-biking trail. Rangers and costumed interpreters are on hand at the visitor center (address left), and rides in old-time boats are also available.

DUMBARTON OAKS

202-339-6401; www.doaks.org; 1703 32nd St NW; 2-6pm Tue-Sun Mar 15-Oct, to 5pm Tue-Sun Nov-Mar 14; admission to collection free, gardens adult/child $5/3

One of the finest mansions in DC is set on some of its finest gardens, a multiterraced study in pruned elegance that's gorgeous any time of year. Nineteen ponds and pools

The stately mansion at Dumbarton Oaks estate, a treasure trove of Byzantine and pre-Columbian art

THE STAIRMASTER... FROM HELL

Across from the Key Bridge is a steep set of stairs that happens to be 1) a popular track for joggers and 2) the spot where demonically possessed Regan of *The Exorcist* sent victims to their screaming deaths. Come on foggy nights, when the steps really are creepy as hell, and don't try and walk them drunk (trust us). The actual address is 3600 Prospect St NW (there was an Exxon station next door at the time of research), and by NW, we mean the northwest quadrant of... hell! Mwa ha ha – er, sorry.

are dolloped over 16 acres of landscaped goodness. In the mansion itself is a collection of fine Byzantine and pre-Columbian art, and, as a bonus, this is where folks decided to found the UN in 1944.

GEORGETOWN UNIVERSITY

☎ 202-687-6538; www.georgetown.edu; 37th & O St NW

These attractive grounds house some of America's best and brightest students, lecturers (Madeleine Albright) and alumni (Hillary and Bill Clinton). It's a party place too; Georgetown's student body gives the surrounding 'hood its distinctive verve. The nation's first Catholic university was founded by the country's first black Jesuit, Patrick Healy, in 1789.

GEORGETOWN WATERFRONT PARK

☎ 202-334-2000; 2100 C St NW; Ⓜ Foggy Bottom-GWU

A new park is revamping the once blah waterfront with lanes of pedestrian-friendly cuteness, shady trees and general green sensibility. The grounds are a bit of a work in progress, but thanks to the above effort it's already become a pleasant place for an evening summer stroll along the Potomac.

OLD STONE HOUSE

☎ 202-426-6851; www.nps.gov/rocr; 3051 M St; admission free; noon-5pm Wed-Sun

The capital's oldest surviving building has been a tavern, brothel and boardinghouse (sometimes all at once), and today, despite sitting in the middle of M St, serves as a garden and peek into 18th-century American life.

SHOP

BIG PLANET COMICS *Books*

☎ 202-342-1961; 3145 Dumbarton St NW; 11am-7pm Mon, Tue, Thu & Fri, to 8pm Wed, to 6pm Sat, noon-5pm Sun

Not to peddle in ugly stereotypes, but this must be one of the first comic book stores we've been in (and this Dungeons and Dragons–loving author – yeah, that's right – has seen a lot) where the clientele is attractive. But more importantly, it also has an excellent collection of limited editions and graphic novels, although not many table-top RPGs (damn).

CADY'S ALLEY *Design*

www.cadysalley.com; 3318 M St NW; vary per store

Not a store per se, Cady's Alley is exactly that, a small street lined with ubercool (and often expensive) interior-design boutiques selling everything from concept furniture to faucets of the future.

LANTERN *Books*

202-333-3222; 3241 P St NW; 11am-4pm Tue-Fri, to 5pm Sat, noon-5pm Sun

These dusty shelves conceal a lovely collection of used books and maps. It's the perfect sort of spot to while away a windy, autumn Georgetown afternoon.

PROPER TOPPER *Gifts*

202-333-6200; www.propertopper.com; 3213 P St NW; 10:30am-6:30pm Mon-Fri, 10am-7pm Sat, noon-6pm Sun

A little bit vintage, a lot chic boutique, this is where discerning Hoyas (Georgetown students) get outfitted and accessorized. In point of fact, while the clothes are nice, the jewelry, handbags and gifts, of the flapper-girl-on-the-town school of style, are the big sell here.

RELISH *Clothing*

202-333-5343; www.relishdc.com; 3312 Cady's Alley NW; 10am-6pm Mon-Wed, Fri & Sat, to 7pm Thu

This author will happily admit his inherent guy-ness to all, but even he knows the best boutique around when he sees it. Jill Platner, Nicole Farhi and other names – that make some scrunch their eyebrows and savvy shoppers salivate – line the racks of this pinnacle of the DC fashion-favored scene.

TUGOOH TOYS *Gifts*

202-654-2412; 1419 Wisconsin Ave NW; 10am-6pm Mon-Sat, noon-5pm Sun

If you've ever been nostalgic for the great wooden toys of childhood (the ones with excellent bite marks), find them done up dazzling for the 21st century in this hip wonderland. That said, the staff can sometimes seem to get impatient with wee ones – odd, considering this store isn't exactly aimed at an adult demographic.

EAT

1789 *American* $$$

202-347-5732; www.1789restaurant.com; 1226 36th St NW; 6-10pm Mon-Thu, to 11pm Fri, 5:30-11pm Sat & Sun

This was one of the first high-end geniuses of the 'rustic New American' genre, so if you're going to try local ingredients sexed up with provincial flair (think Virginia rabbit in seasonal sauce), this is the spot to indulge. Formal wear (jacket) is not only expected, but required for dinner.

BAKED & WIRED *Café* $

☎ 202-333-2500; www.bakedandwired.com; 1052 Thomas Jefferson St NW; 6am-7pm Mon-Fri, 9am-7pm Sat, 11am-5pm Sun

With one of the nation's great universities a cappuccino away, you'd think Georgetown would have more hip coffee shops, but alas, there's a lack. B&W makes up for this lost ground with a studio-chic interior and, more importantly, great coffee and some of the best cupcakes in DC.

CAFÉ MILANO *European* $$$

☎ 202-333-6183; www.cafemilano.net; 1331 H St NW; 11:30am-11pm Sun-Tue, to midnight Wed-Sat

Widely regarded by locals as one of the best bring-your-date-out-for-some-upscale-Italian eateries in Washington, DC, Milano has been racking up political bigwigs and besotted Georgetown couples for years with its excellent executions of northern Italian favorites.

CITRONELLE *Modern* $$$

☎ 202-625-2150; www.citronelledc.com; 3000 M St NW; 6-9:30pm

Big name Michel Richard started this show, a split-level study in the most creative twists tweakable on the American palate. Shrimp wrapped in phyllo dough spun from a cloud is a good example of the above, but order anything, and if in doubt, give the tasting menu some love.

HOW TO HOOK UP HERE

Young, winsome interns flood DC with fresh faces and raging hormones every summer, but few realize there's an art to DC dating. You need to come off as connected but not trying to look connected; in with someone who matters but nonchalant; top of your class but unconcerned. Or as a friend puts it, 'Don't act like the douche bag you probably are.' Herein: some tips.

> Were you class president? Big deal. So was everyone else.

> Don't flash your ID badge unless you're absolutely sure it beats the one held by Mr Top Secret Level Clearance over by the jukebox.

> If hitting on Republicans: 'I work for the CIA/DoD (Department of Defense).' For Democrats: Obama transition team = Summer of Love!

> Need a fourth-quarter miracle? If it's 2am and you're flailing, try Wonderland (p103), Marvin (p86) or anywhere on 18th St (p113).

WORTH THE TRIP

The slew of suburbs that sprawls on the west bank of the Potomac contains some of DC's most impressive sights – technically not in DC – and thousands of residents who want access to the capital sans its taxes and gridlock. As a result, **Arlington** is both of and distinct from the District, a semisatellite hanging in Washington's orbit. Of all the towns in the amorphous northern Virginia area, Arlington offers the most important agencies and capital ephemera.

The must-see, and one of the most sadly evocative sights in the region (if not country) is **Arlington National Cemetery** (☎ 703-607-8000; www.arlingtoncemetery.org; admission free; 8am-7pm Apr-Sep, to 5pm Oct-Mar; M Arlington Cemetery). Washington's marble often celebrates America's victories and achievements, but this elegiac counterpoint commemorates her loss: specifically, of over 290,000 service members (and dependents) marked by simple white headstones and the left mementos of more than four million annual visitors. Be on the lookout for the Marine Corps Memorial (displaying the famous raising of the flag over Mt Suribachi), the Tomb of the Unknowns and the Eternal Flame for John F Kennedy.

Still a symbol of American power (and, following 9/11, vulnerability and rebuilding), the **Pentagon & Pentagon Memorial** (☎ 703-695-1776; http://pentagon.afis.osd.mil; tours by reservation only 9am-3pm Mon-Fri; M Pentagon) lie just over the Potomac from the capital. One of the largest office buildings in the world stretches five floors up and five floors down, via 17.5 miles of corridors that house the US Department of Defense. Civilians can arrange tours through their relevant congressperson or, if a foreign national, embassy. The tranquil memorial to the 184 victims of the 9/11 attacks (including Pentagon staff and passengers of American Airlines Flight 77) consists of 184 benches each engraved with a victim's name, shaded by 85 paperback maple trees.

Arlington's eating scene has long been thriving, spurred along by the presence of countless bedroom-suburb commuters who desire DC's eating quality without the hassle of living downtown. When they need meat between buns, they pop down to **Ray's Hell Burger** (☎ 703-841-0001; 1713 Wilson Blvd; noon-10pm Tue-Sun, from 5pm Mon; M Rosslyn). Do Ray's (hell) burgers taste as good as they sound? Hell yes. What makes them hellish(ly good)? The free jalapeños, and the massive amounts of meat, and the way the meat drip kinda melts the bun the way your dad's burgers did, and any of the stupendous cheeses you can melt on that bad boy. Ray: we salute you.

We can't sign off on Arlington without shipping you a few miles west to the corner of Wilson Blvd in **Seven Sisters**, VA. Here you'll find a slice of Saigon masquerading as a strip mall: the Eden Center, heart of the Washington area's Vietnamese community. There's traditional medicine, mah-jongg tables, fresh Southeast Asian produce and a vibe that's more south Vietnam than northern Virginia. If you need some *pho* (noodle soup), pop into any restaurant here and emerge smiling.

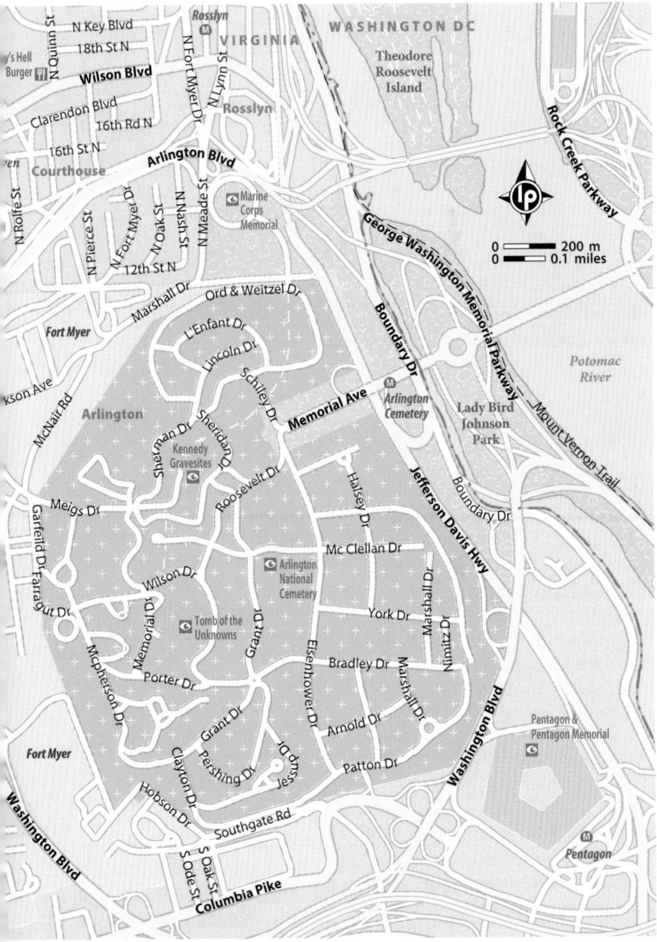
WASHINGTON DC
VIRGINIA
Theodore Roosevelt Island
Rosslyn
Courthouse
Marine Corps Memorial
Fort Myer
Arlington
Kennedy Gravesites
Arlington Cemetery
Lady Bird Johnson Park
Potomac River
Arlington National Cemetery
Tomb of the Unknowns
Pentagon & Pentagon Memorial
Pentagon
Fort Myer
Wilson Blvd
Arlington Blvd
Clarendon Blvd
N Key Blvd
18th St N
16th Rd N
16th St N
12th St N
N Fort Myer Dr
N Lynn St
N Meade St
N Nash St
N Oak St
N Pierce St
N Rolfe St
N Quinn St
Marshall Dr
Ord & Weitzel Dr
L'Enfant Dr
Lincoln Dr
Schiley Dr
Sheridan Dr
Sherman Dr
Memorial Ave
Boundary Dr
George Washington Memorial Parkway
Rock Creek Parkway
Mount Vernon Trail
Jefferson Davis Hwy
Roosevelt Dr
Halsey Dr
Meigs Dr
Garfeild Dr
Farragut Dr
McNair Rd
Mc Clellan Dr
Wilson Dr
York Dr
Marshall Dr
Nimitz Dr
Memorial Dr
Grant Dr
Eisenhower Dr
Bradley Dr
Porter Dr
Mcpherson Dr
Arnold Dr
Patton Dr
Jessup Dr
Pershing Dr
Clayton Dr
Hobson Dr
Southgate Rd
Washington Blvd
Columbia Pike
S Oak St
S Ode St
200 m
0.1 miles

The simple facade of Blues Alley belies the jazz greats who perform within

HOOK *Seafood* $$$

☎ 202-625-4488; www.hookdc.com; 3241 M St NW; 11:30am-2:30pm Tue-Fri, 11am-2:30pm Sat & Sun, 5-10pm Sun-Tue, to 11pm Wed-Sat
Simple and sexy, with a frosty white Zen interior, Hook is the fish bar of the future. Locally sourced seafood is prepped artfully yet simply, so the flesh of your flounder or rockfish is allowed to play, with just the right nudge in the direction of deliciousness.

MARTIN'S TAVERN *American* $

☎ 202-333-7370; www.martins-tavern.com; 1264 Wisconsin Ave NW; 11am-1:30am Mon-Thu, to 2:30am Fri, 9am-2:30am Sat, 8am-1:30am Sun
Forget the fact JFK popped the question to Jackie in booth number three, or the power lunches that have haunted this dark-wood wonder – all of the above is great context, but only window dressing to a cold beer and the best cheeseburger in town.

DRINK

MIE N YU *Lounge*

☎ 202-333-6122; www.mienyu.com; 3125 M St NW; 5-11pm Mon & Tue, 11:30am-11pm Wed & Thu, 11:30am-midnight Fri & Sat, 11am-11pm Sun

Georgetown's most popular lounge bar is also a Middle Eastern–Mediterranean-Asian fusion restaurant, but we come to see really, really good-looking people sip really, really expensive drinks.

MR SMITH'S *Dive*

☎ 202-333-3104; 3104 M St NW; 11:30am-2am Mon-Thu, to 3am Fri & Sat, 11am-2am Sun

This is as divey as they come in Georgetown – sawdust and dusky interior concealing patrons that only get more rowdy and roaring with the night. That said, Mr Smith's is as popular with Georgetown Jonathan as Average Joe, which makes for an intriguing and generally affable atmosphere.

TOMBS *Pub*

☎ 202-337-6668; 1226 36th St NW; 11:30am-1:15am Mon-Thu, to 2:30am Fri & Sat, from 9:30am Sun

Every school of a certain pedigree has 'that' bar – the one where faculty and students alike sip pints and play darts under athletic regalia of the old school. Tombs is Georgetown's contribution to the genre, and also happened to be a shooting set for *St Elmo's Fire*.

PLAY

BLUES ALLEY *Jazz Bar*

☎ 202-337-4141; www.bluesalley.com; 1073 Wisconsin Ave NW; 6pm-12:30am

Calling the Alley an establishment is like calling the Lincoln Memorial a landmark. If you grew up around the way, your parents likely went on dates here to watch greats like Dizzy Gillespie back in the day. The talent is just as sterling these days, and the setting just as sophisticated.

>U STREET & SHAW

The history of this neighborhood makes for a neat little analogy of Washington as a whole. 'Before Harlem, there was Shaw,' the black Renaissance redoubt that made DC a beating heart of African American culture during the early 20th century. Then came neglect, decay, the 1968 riots and open-air drug markets, which later gave way to the 1990s and gentrification. Cheap rents reeled in restaurants, artists, clubs and creative types, until it became what it is today: a 'hood that straddles all of DC's many fault lines.

To the joy of some and chagrin of others, the U St corridor west of Shaw, and increasingly, Shaw itself, may be what Washington, DC is becoming: the capital mixed, where older black communities have shrunk but not disappeared, new white-occupied condo complexes are sprouting and Latinos hold rocking karaoke nights in the midst of everything. Imperfect? Sure. Fun? Hell yes. Worth checking out? More like: why aren't you here already?

U STREET & SHAW

SEE

African American Civil War Memorial 1 C2
African American Civil War Museum 2 C3
Founders' Library 3 D1
Howard University 4 D1
Howard University Gallery of Art ..... (see 4)

SHOP

Circle Boutique 5 B3
Dekka 6 B2
Hunted House 7 B3
Legendary Beast 8 A2
Nana ..... (see 8)
Redeem 9 B3
U Street Flea Market 10 C3

EAT

Ben's Chili Bowl 11 C2
Busboys & Poets 12 B2
Cork 13 B3
Crème 14 B2
Florida Avenue Grill 15 C2
Judy's 16 B2
Soul Vegetarian Restaurant 17 D1
Vegetate 18 C4

DRINK

Café St-Ex 19 B3
Marvin 20 B2
Saloon 21 C3
Stetson's 22 A2

PLAY

9:30 Club 23 C2
Black Cat 24 B3
Bohemian Caverns 25 C2
Lincoln Theatre 26 C2
Local 16 ..... 27 A2
Republic Gardens 28 B2

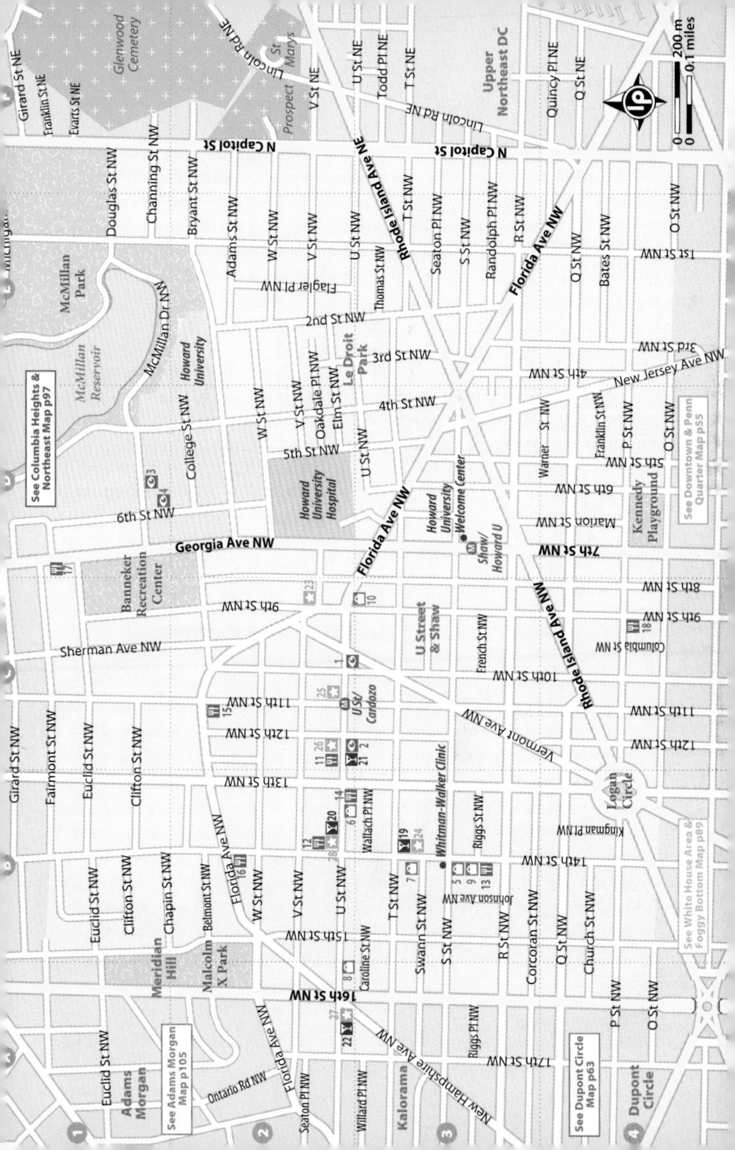

Upper Northeast DC
U Street & Shaw
Le Droit Park
Howard University
Howard University Hospital
Howard University Welcome Center
Shaw/Howard U
U St/Cardozo
Whitman-Walker Clinic
Banneker Recreation Center
Kennedy Playground
McMillan Park
McMillan Reservoir
Glenwood Cemetery
Prospect
St Marys
Logan Circle
Meridian Hill
Malcolm X Park
Adams Morgan
Kalorama
Dupont Circle
See Columbia Heights & Northeast Map p97
See Adams Morgan Map p105
See Dupont Circle Map p63
See White House Area & Foggy Bottom Map p89
See Downtown & Penn Quarter Map p55
Georgia Ave NW
Florida Ave NW
Rhode Island Ave NW
Rhode Island Ave NE
New Jersey Ave NW
New Hampshire Ave NW
Vermont Ave NW
Sherman Ave NW
Lincoln Rd NE
N Capitol St
16th St NW
7th St NW
200 m
0.1 miles

SEE

All places listed in this chapter are served by the U Street-Cardozo/ African American Civil War Memorial Metro, unless otherwise noted.

AFRICAN AMERICAN CIVIL WAR MEMORIAL & MUSEUM

☎ 202-667-2667; www.afroamcivilwar.org; memorial U St & Vermont Ave NW, museum 1200 U St NW; admission free; 10am-5pm Mon-Fri, to 2pm Sat
Over 200,000 free blacks and former slaves served in the Union Army during the Civil War. This memorial and museum marks their contribution and makes the point that while for some, the war was fought over secession versus union, for others, it was a matter of breaking human bondage. Besides a permanent exhibition on the above, the museum has a searchable database of enlisted Civil War–era ancestors.

HOWARD UNIVERSITY

☎ 202-806-6100; www.howard.edu; 2400 6th St NW; M Shaw-Howard U
Arguably the best traditionally African American university in America dominates Shaw and Georgia Ave. You'll want to visit the Georgian-style Founders' Library, and the **Howard University Gallery of Art** (admission free; 9:30am-4pm Mon-Fri), showcasing African and African

On campus at traditionally African American Howard University

THE SOUL OF U STREET

Langston Hughes would have loved DC in the early 20th century – a quick list of names and venues is proof U St and Shaw could have given Harlem a run for its money. **Bohemian Caverns** (p87) headlined Ella Fitzgerald; Pearl Bailey danced at **Republic Gardens** (U & 15th Sts) when she wasn't waiting tables there; Louis Armstrong played the **Dance Hall** (V & 9th Sts), now closed; Duke Ellington grew up on T St; and all of the above played or saw shows at the **Lincoln Theater** (1215 U St).

American artists. Howard alumni include Toni Morrison, Thurgood Marshall and Ralph Bunche.

SHOP

CIRCLE BOUTIQUE *Clothing*

☎ 202-518-2212; www.circleboutique.com; 1736 14th St NW; noon-7pm Tue-Fri, 11am-7pm Sat, noon-6pm Sun

Girls drag boyfriends here, both to shop for indie chic of the Zen-with-a-dash-of-sexy school, and because Circle has an excellent range of designer menswear you'll not find elsewhere in the capital.

DEKKA *Artists Co-op*

☎ 202-986-1370; www.dekkadesign.com; 1338 U St NW; 9am-5pm Mon-Fri, noon-7pm Sat & Sun

This artists co-op showcases painting, clothing and jewelry produced by Washington-area designers for a loving, local audience. There are few other places in town where you get the palpable sense that DC is growing out of its navy-blue suit into the funky beast she always wanted to be.

HUNTED HOUSE

Vintage Homewares

☎ 202-549-7493; www.huntedhousedc.com; 1830 14th St NW; 1-7pm Thu, noon-6pm Fri, 11am-6pm Sat & Sun, by appointment Tue

Every piece of vintage furniture stuffing this walk-up, laid out to resemble a functioning apartment (like, the most awesome apartment ever) is a gem of the deco or modernism design movement. We could spend hours staring at the Jetsons-esque TV in the sitting room, which is heart-achingly never for sale.

LEGENDARY BEAST *Gifts*

☎ 202-797-1234; www.legendarybeast.com; 1520 U St; 9am-5pm Mon-Fri, noon-7pm Sat & Sun

'I run the mom shop,' says the DC-area born-and-bred owner of this magical attic, and we suppose she's right – if mom were the kind of gal who was into Tibetan jewelry, Egyptian scarabs and homemade shrines to Johnny Depp.

NANA *Clothing*

202-667-6955; www.nanadc.com; 1528 U St; noon-7pm Mon-Sat, to 5pm Sun

This locally owned boutique is almost as cute as the artsy jewelry under the glass or belted dresses, chunky belts, checkered coats and butt-hugging (but purse-friendly) jeans gracing the racks.

REDEEM *Clothing*

202-332-7447; www.redeemus.com; 1734 14th St NW; noon-8pm Mon-Sat, to 6pm Sun

It helps that Redeem's black, white and shades-of-gray outfits are exemplars of monochrome cool (offset with splashes of color and bling depending on the season). But this socially conscious store goes the extra mile via public parties for charities and support for local artists and designers. Do good; shop stylishly; redeem thyself.

U STREET FLEA MARKET *Flea Market*

cnr U & 9th Sts; noon-8pm Sat & Sun

You won't (likely) find a cute vintage frock here; this is a real flea market, for people who second-hand shop out of necessity rather than as a diversion. That said, there are usually awesome albums for sale, a few local crafts and a sense of U St's vibe circa 1980s BG (Before Gentrification).

EAT

BEN'S CHILI BOWL

American $

202-667-0909; www.benschilibowl.com; 1213 U St; noon-4am

Ben's Chili Bowl is to DC dining what the White House is to DC sightseeing. Opened and operated by Ben Ali and family (you may notice that it's adjacent to Ben Ali Lane), the Bowl's main stock in trade is half smokes, DC's meatier, smokier (duh) version of the hot dog, which is usually served slathered in mustard and helpings of the namesake chili. Until recently, Bill Cosby was the only person who ate for free here, but now Barack Obama apparently gets the comp nod, too.

BUSBOYS & POETS

American $

202-387-7638; www.busboysandpoets.com; 2021 14th St NW; 8am-midnight Mon-Thu, 8am-2am Fri, 9am-2am Sat, 9am-midnight Sun

In just a few years, Busboys (named for a Langston Hughes poem) has become a U St stalwart. A black-owned business, it's where everyone seems to gather for coffee, wi-fi, café fare and a progressive vibe (and attached bookstore) that makes San Francisco feel conservative.

CORK *Small Plates* $$$

☎ 202-387-1462; www.corkdc.com; 1720 14th St NW; 5pm-1am; M U Street-Cardozo or Dupont Circle

This dark 'n' cozy wine bar manages to come off as foodie magnet and friendly neighborhood hangout all at once, which is a feat. Smart wine choices plus small plates equal culinary bliss – with this innovative menu (and excellent cheese selection) you generally can't go wrong, although those little dishes do add up on the wallet.

CRÈME *Soul* $$

☎ 202-234-1884; http://cremedc.com; 1322 U St; 6-10:30pm Mon-Thu, to 11:30pm Fri & Sat, 11am-3pm Sat, 10am-3:30pm & 6-10:30pm Sun

Crème's upscale soul attracts a multiculti crowd and is particularly popular with buppies (black yuppies), who enjoy a stick-to-your-ribs menu served in a slick dining room of beiges and buffed metal. Fight for seats at Sunday brunch; the chicken and waffles might be our favorite morning-after nosh in DC.

FLORIDA AVENUE GRILL *American* $

☎ 202-265-1586; 1100 Florida Ave NW; 11:30am-9pm Tue-Sat

Besides the Hitching Post (p101), we deem the Grill DC's quintessential diner. Be they president, Harlem Globetrotter or college student, they've all come here for almost 70 years to eat turkey legs, catfish and meatloaf served with sides of sweet tea and more character than Shakespeare's collected works.

Share tasty tapas and top drops at cozy Cork

JUDY'S *Latin American* $

☎ 202-265-2519; 2212 14th St NW; 9am-midnight

When we asked a Honduran friend where to get good Central American food, her unhesitating answer was: 'Judy's.' Everything's good, but the breakfasts, consisting of tamales, white cheese and other odds and ends, are tops. Come at night for the best Spanish karaoke in town.

BEST BEER GARDENS

Washington's sweltering summer makes outdoor drinking divine. Here's a list of our favorite spots for an alfresco tipple:

> Marvin (right)
> Stetson's (opposite)
> Looking Glass Lounge (p102)
> Big Hunt (p67)
> Wonderland (p103)

SOUL VEGETARIAN RESTAURANT *Vegetarian* $

202-328-7685; 2606 Georgia Ave; 11am-9pm Mon-Sat, to 3pm Sun; M Shaw/Howard-U

'Soul food' plus 'vegetarian' aren't generally two values added together in dining arithmetic, but along comes this cool hideaway. There's inevitably a guy with dreads enjoying some of the best yams ya' ever stuffed your face with or something off the impressive, gut-busting (really!) vegan menu.

VEGETATE *Vegetarian* $$

202-232-4585; www.vegetatedc.com; 1414 9th St NW; 6-10pm Tue-Thu, to 10:30pm Fri, 5-10:30pm Sat

As you read, probably the best vegetarian food in town is being served here: blue cheese skillet bread and bambi-friendly risottos, all prepped with ingredients culled from local farms. You enter, you eat, you leave, feeling good about your meal, your karma, your place in the circle of delicious life.

DRINK

CAFÉ ST-EX *Lounge*

202-265-7839; 1847 14th St NW; 5:30pm-1am Sun-Wed, to 2am Thu-Sat

This spot's outdoor chalkboard once read: 'No Popped Collars.' We kinda fell in love with it right away. It's still hip, even a little preppy, stuffed with a weird French-aviation theme underlaid by a basement bar/dance club that gets sweaty and fairly hormonal as the night wears on.

MARVIN *Lounge*

202-797-7171; www.marvindc.com; 2007 14th St NW; 5:30pm-2am

One of our favorite watering holes is always good for playing hottie spotty, but it's hardly intimidating. The roof deck is great for rubbing shoulders and sparking conversation on summer nights or in the midst of winter, when folks huddle under roaring heat lamps and enjoy imported Belgian beer.

SALOON *Beerstravaganza*

202-462-2640; 1207 U St NW; 11am-11pm Tue-Thu, to 2am Fri & Sat

The Saloon takes a firm stand against packing patrons in like sardines, with posted rules against standing between tables. That's great, because the added elbow room better allows you to enjoy brew ordered off one of the most extensive beer menus in town.

STETSON'S *Bar*

☎ 202-667-6295; 1610 U St NW; 5pm-2am

Stetson's is a political spot and not. There's a good chance you'll be hanging with Senate staffers, but folks don't flash congressional ID badges here: they come for beer, peanuts, fun times and no flash. The beer garden is a bonus.

PLAY

9:30 CLUB *Live Music*

☎ 202-393-0930; www.930.com; 815 V St NW; from 7:30pm Sun-Thu

For years this intimate (for a 1200-seat warehouse) venue has been one of DC's premier spots for seeing both big names (Justin Timberlake) and obscure indie (some Swedish folk-rock set, last we remember).

BLACK CAT *Live Music*

☎ 202-667-7960; www.blackcatdc.com; 1811 14th St NW

Still one of the best places in town for rock or indie, the Cat also always keeps something good going on the back stage, from soul funk nights to heavy metal dance-offs to big-band-era bashes.

BOHEMIAN CAVERNS *Jazz Bar*

☎ 202-299-0800; www.bohemiancaverns.com; 2003 11th St NW; 6pm-2am Wed-Sat

One of Washington's most pedigreed grand dames reopened in 2000; before, it hosted the likes of Miles, Coltrane, Ellington and Ella. There are frequent open mic nights and an increasing crop of names headlining to reestablish the title of this icon of American jazz.

LOCAL 16 *Lounge*

☎ 202-265-2828; http://local16.com; 1602 U St NW

Weekend nights find Local 16 consistently packed with DC's hot to trot, usually decked to the nines (or showing off some skin), trading drinks and winks over two floors of nightlife fun. In summers, the outdoor balcony is popular – and crowded – as hell.

>WHITE HOUSE AREA & FOGGY BOTTOM

The White House, cocooned in a clot of neoclassical, Federal, Victorian and jazz age architecture, draws visitors north of the Mall like moths to a pale flame. In the immediate vicinity of America's most important address are Farragut, McPherson and Lafayette Squares, where fine restaurants (along with many homeless) are spread around the line that divides DC's 'new' Downtown from Foggy Bottom.

The latter derives its name from both its low-lying geography, which serves as a catchment for Potomac mists, and the clouds of smoke that emanated from the heavy industry once concentrated here. Today Foggy Bottom is synonymous with the State Department, World Bank, IMF and other institutions that give this area an internationally important, if overtly corporate, atmosphere.

This is an area that rewards those seeking fine dining and old architecture, and those who want that sense of DC's finger on the pulse of power.

WHITE HOUSE AREA & FOGGY BOTTOM

SEE

- Corcoran Gallery of Art 1 D3
- Lafayette Square 2 E2
- Octagon Museum 3 D3
- Renwick Gallery 4 E2
- St John's Church 5 E2
- Watergate 6 A2
- White House 7 E3
- White House Visitor Center 8 F3

SHOP

- ADC Map & Travel Center 9 E2
- Pangea 10 C2

EAT

- 14K 11 F2
- Café Mozart 12 F2
- DC Coast 13 F2
- Founding Farmers 14 D2
- Georgia Brown's 15 E2
- Kinkead's 16 C2
- Old Ebbitt Grill 17 F3
- Prime Rib 18 C2
- Sichuan Pavilion 19 D2

DRINK

- Froggy Bottom Pub 20 C2

PLAY

- Kennedy Center 21 A3

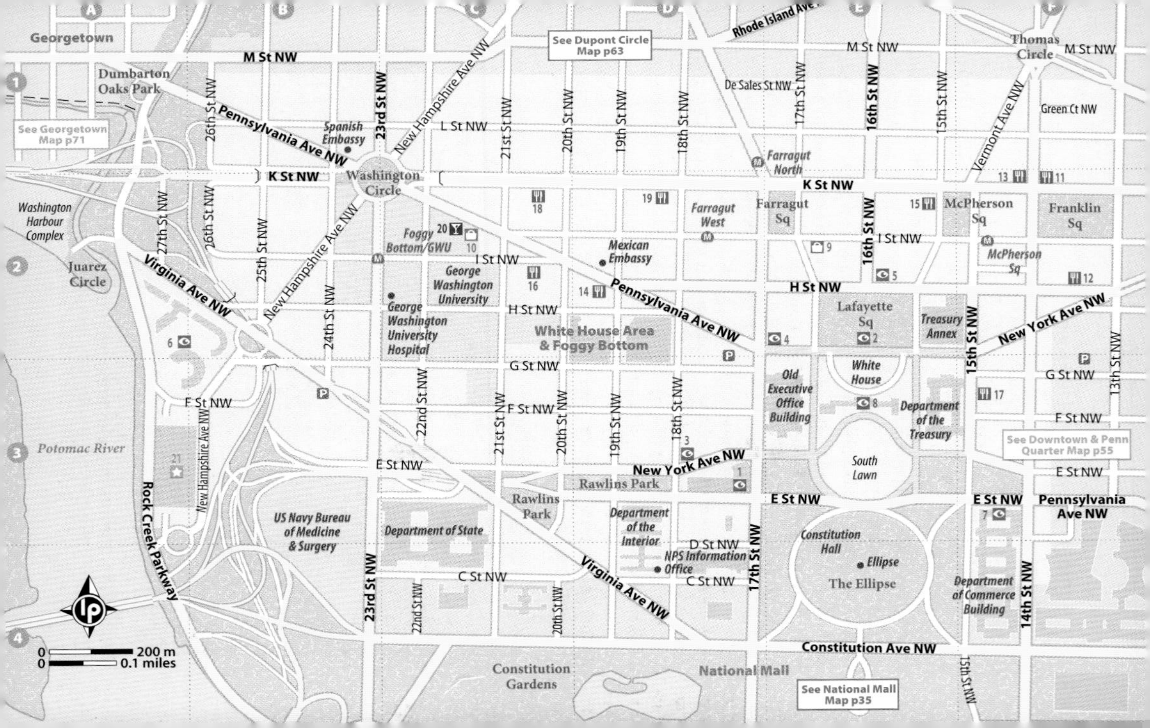

Georgetown
Dumbarton Oaks Park
See Georgetown Map p71
See Dupont Circle Map p63
See Downtown & Penn Quarter Map p55
See National Mall Map p35
Washington Harbour Complex
Juarez Circle
Potomac River
Rock Creek Parkway
Washington Circle
Thomas Circle
Spanish Embassy
Mexican Embassy
Foggy Bottom/GWU
Farragut West
Farragut North
Farragut Sq
McPherson Sq
Franklin Sq
Lafayette Sq
Treasury Annex
White House
Old Executive Office Building
Department of the Treasury
South Lawn
Constitution Hall
Ellipse
The Ellipse
Department of Commerce Building
George Washington University
George Washington University Hospital
White House Area & Foggy Bottom
Rawlins Park
Department of the Interior
NPS Information Office
Department of State
US Navy Bureau of Medicine & Surgery
Constitution Gardens
National Mall
M St NW
L St NW
K St NW
I St NW
H St NW
G St NW
F St NW
E St NW
D St NW
C St NW
De Sales St NW
Green Ct NW
Rhode Island Ave
Vermont Ave NW
New Hampshire Ave NW
Pennsylvania Ave NW
Virginia Ave NW
New York Ave NW
Constitution Ave NW
13th St NW
14th St NW
15th St NW
16th St NW
17th St NW
18th St NW
19th St NW
20th St NW
21st St NW
22nd St NW
23rd St NW
24th St NW
25th St NW
26th St NW
27th St NW
200 m
0.1 miles

SEE

CORCORAN GALLERY OF ART

☎ 202-639-1700; www.corcoran.org; 500 17th St NW; general admission $6, special exhibitions $14; 10am-5pm Wed & Fri-Sun, to 9pm Thu; M Farragut West

You'd think the largest private museum in the city couldn't compare to the Smithsonian – and you'd think wrong. The Corcoran's permanent gallery of American, European and contemporary art is grand enough, but special exhibitions, especially the theses projects culled from the Corcoran's own school of design, are the real standout.

LAFAYETTE SQUARE

Pennsylvania Ave btwn 15th & 17th St NW; M Farragut West

The four corners of this green plot just north of the White House are held down by statues of volunteer foreigners who joined the American Revolution and rose to prominence in rebel ranks. Look out for the Marquis de Lafayette, who became a general at the age of 19, and Polish Tadeusz Kosciusko, who went on to lead uprisings in his homeland against Imperial Russia.

OCTAGON MUSEUM

☎ 202-638-3221; www.archfoundation.org/octagon; 1799 New York Ave NW; M Farragut West

'Honey, I'm home!' Chopper coming in to land in front of the president's big White House

VISITING THE WHITE HOUSE

To get into the White House you either need to a) work there, b) be elected president, c) get invited, or d) be an American citizen or resident and come on a public tour with a group of 10 or more. If you don't have enough heads, try anyway; sometimes groups are combined. You'll need to make a request through your Member of Congress up to six months in advance; tours are usually confirmed a month beforehand. The tour itself is self-guided and runs from 7:30am to 12:30pm Tuesday to Saturday; call ☎ 202-456-7041 for details.

The apex of the Federal style of architecture pioneered in the USA also happens to be the oldest museum in America dedicated to architecture and design. Run by the American Architectural Foundation, the house was closed for renovation at the time of press, but should be open by the time you read this; tours can be arranged through the phone number listed left.

RENWICK GALLERY

☎ 202-633-1000; www.americanart.si.edu; 1661 Pennsylvania Ave NW; admission free; 10am-5:30pm; M Farragut West

Part of the Smithsonian American Art Museum, the Renwick highlights the rich tradition of American decorative arts and crafts. The gorgeous Grand Salon is decked with paintings from the American Art Museum's main galleries.

ST JOHN'S CHURCH

☎ 202-347-8766; 1525 H St NW; M Farragut West/McPherson Sq

Pale yellow and more humble than haughty, this cozy Episcopal church has nonetheless counted every president since James Madison as at least an occasional attendee; the 54th pew is reserved for the commander-in-chief.

WATERGATE

☎ 202-965-2300; www.thewatergatehotel.com; 2650 Virginia Ave NW; M Foggy Bottom-GWU

The Watergate has housed the likes of Monica Lewinsky, Ruth Bader Ginsburg and Condoleezza Rice, and was, of course, the site of the Watergate break-ins. The '60s modernist hotel looms over Foggy Bottom; it was closed for renovations as of press time, but should reopen by the time you read this.

WHITE HOUSE

☎ 202-456-1414; www.whitehouse.gov; 1600 Pennsylvania Ave NW; M Farragut West

It doesn't matter how many times you've seen it on TV, the first time you spot the White House with

SCANDAL SITES

Put the power-hungry, those attracted to the power-hungry, those attracted to those attracted to the power-hungry, professional dirt-artists and several thousand journalists in one city and you get: scandal. Some of our favorite places for DC misbehavior:

> The Watergate (for obvious reasons)
> Vista Hotel (now called the Wyndham Washington Hotel) – where former mayor Marion Barry got caught with crack and ex-model turned police informant Hazel 'Rasheeda' Moore and said, bless him, 'Bitch set me up!'
> Something parking garage, space 113 – where Robert Woodward had secret meetings with W Mark Felt, also known as 'Deep Throat,' his informant on the Watergate scandal.
> Pentagon City Food Court – the sushi bar in this northern Virginia mall is where Monica Lewinsky awaited Linda Tripp, who betrayed the intern to federal investigator Ken Starr.

your own eyes, it's gasp-worthy. The president's home screams dignity, pomp and circumstance, and on cold nights, shimmers with ghostly luminescence. For all that, this is a home and every occupant has added their touch, from Jackie Kennedy's interior revamp to Grant's zoo to Clinton's jogging track. Getting inside can be tough (see p91), but the **White House visitor center** (☎ 202-208-1631; www.nps.gov/whho; 1450 Pennsylvania Ave NW; 🕓 7:30am-4pm) gives you a good taste.

SHOP

ADC MAP & TRAVEL CENTER *Books*

☎ 202-628-2608; 1636 I St NW; Ⓜ McPherson Sq

If you need any sort of map or travel guide, it can probably be found at this little shop, which caters to Lonely Planet aficionados (and anyone who loves the open road) par excellence.

PANGEA *Gifts*

☎ 202-628-2608; 2121 Pennsylvania Ave NW; Ⓜ Foggy Bottom-GWU

This very cool crafts emporium sells artisan work from around the globe, particularly from developing countries. Profits are reinvested into local communities, and best of all, when you're done you can have a bracing cup of fair-trade coffee.

EAT

14K *American* $$$

☎ 202-218-7575; www.14krestaurant.com; 1001 14th St NW; 🕓 6:30am-11pm Mon-Fri, from 7am Sat & Sun; Ⓜ McPherson Sq

It's lunchtime on K St, Mr Lobbyist. You've got an hour to impress but not go over the top. Solution? One of the excellent sandwiches (we like the turkey griller) at this sleek-chic New American bistro. Skip the overpriced dinners.

CAFÉ MOZART *European* $$

☎ 202-347-5732; www.cafemozartgermandeli.com; 1331 H St NW; 7am-10pm Mon-Fri, from 9am Sat, from 11am Sun; Ⓜ Metro Center

Got spaetzle? Schnitzel? Come here, Klaus, to this rather excellent German grocery store with a nice restaurant in the back that hosts (wait for it) accordion concerts on Tuesdays and Sundays and opera nights on Wednesdays.

DC COAST *Seafood* $$$

☎ 202-216-5988; www.dccoast.com; 1401 K St NW; 11:30am-2:30pm & 5:30-10:30pm Mon-Thu, to 11pm Fri & Sat; Ⓜ McPherson Sq

One of DC's most famous seafood spots; seared yellowfin and bass wrapped in pancetta are served in a Poseidon's temple of a dining room, half over-the-top opulence, half crisp table-clothed class.

FOUNDING FARMERS *American* $$

☎ 202-822-8783; www.wearefoundingfarmers.com; 1925 Pennsylvania Ave NW; 8am-10pm Mon-Wed, to 11pm Thu & Fri, 4-11pm Sat, 10am-9pm Sun; Ⓜ Farragut West

They serve 'bacon cocktails' here. No, really. And they're awesome, as is the frosty decor of pickled goods in jars overlooking an art gallery of a dining space, a combination of made-from-scratch and modern art that reflects the nature of the locally sourced, New American food (figs, prosciutto, fried chicken, and ricotta ravioli with creamed corn).

GEORGIA BROWN'S *Southern* $$$

☎ 202-393-4499; www.gbrowns.com; 950 15th St NW; 11:30am-10pm Mon-Thu, to 11pm Fri, 5-11pm Sat, 10am-2:30pm & 5:30-10pm Sun; Ⓜ McPherson Sq

One of our favorite restaurants in DC is also one of the city's standards, a flag bearer for New Southern classics cooked in

Well-worn bar stools say it all: Old Ebbitt Grill (p94)

low-country style in a warm, autumnal interior. Come for shrimp on grits like silk, chicken fried into ethereal crispiness and a Sunday brunch Bill Clinton swore by.

KINKEAD'S *Seafood* $$$

☎ 202-296-7700; www.kinkead.com; 2000 Pennsylvania Ave NW; 🕐 11:30am-2:30pm & 5:30-10pm Mon-Fri, 5:30-10pm Sat & Sun; Ⓜ Farragut West

Classy restaurants pop like corn in this town, but Kinkead's is a classic, serving specialties such as cornmeal-crusted flounder that have been keeping executive bigwigs and State Department drones in gastronomic bliss for years.

OLD EBBITT GRILL *American* $$

☎ 202-347-4800; www.ebbitt.com; 675 15th St NW; 🕐 7:30am-1am Mon-Fri, from 8:30am Sat & Sun; Ⓜ McPherson Sq

With its dark wood, mirrored bar and brass accents, fare of trout, pork and steak done up simple and hearty, the Old Ebbitt is good and popular with tourists, journalists and the politicos everyone's trying to spot through the low buzz of the crowd.

PRIME RIB *Steakhouse* $$$

☎ 202-466-8811; www.theprimerib.com; 2020 K St NW; 🕐 11:30am-3pm & 5-10:30pm Mon-Fri, 5-10:30pm Sat; Ⓜ Farragut West

Get dressed to the nines (guys must wear jackets), bring a fat wad of cash (or a powerful credit card) and get ready for some cow, seared perfect, whilst surrounded by DC's power set making the decisions that will determine the future of the nation.

SICHUAN PAVILION *Asian* $

☎ 202-466-7790; http://sichuanpavilion.googlepages.com; 1814 K St NW; 🕐 noon-9pm; Ⓜ Farragut North

Why do we think this may be the best Chinese in the city? Because so many Chinese come here, far from any ethnic enclaves, to dine on excellent, spicy, oily classics of the old school. The *ma pa* tofu is particularly stinky and sublime.

DRINK

FROGGY BOTTOM PUB *Bar*

☎ 202-338-3000; 2141 Pennsylvania Ave NW; 🕐 11:30am-1:30am Sun-Thu, to 2:30am Fri & Sat; Ⓜ Foggy Bottom-GWU

If you're a Patriot (George Washington University student, not lover of thy nation, although they're welcome here too) and haven't stumbled the stairs down to the Froggy's bottom, where you been, man? This is a college bar by every standard of the genre – happy-hour specials, darts, pool, kids getting messy – and in staid and stiff Foggy Bottom, she's all the more welcome for that.

A sun-kissed Kennedy Center on the Potomac River preparing for the evening's performances

PLAY

KENNEDY CENTER

Performing Arts

☎ 202-467-4600; www.kennedy-center.org; 2700 F St NW; Ⓜ Foggy Bottom-GWU

A swirl of ball gowns and slow marches of tuxedo-clad concert goers walk through Washington's most elegant performance hall, which overlooks a bend of the Potomac. The on-site terrace is a supremely romantic place for a drink, or you can take a free tour and catch free concerts on the Millennium Stage every night at 6pm. The National Symphony Orchestra, National Ballet and Washington Chamber Symphony are all based here.

>COLUMBIA HEIGHTS & NORTHEAST

This part of town walks the line closer than Johnny Cash – while U St has already arrived, most of Northeast DC is just pulling into the platform. As a result, you'll find few better examples of what DC traditionally has been and what it could potentially become than these stretches of once outer Washington.

Largely Latino Columbia Heights, rebranded by the new DC as USA Mall, is already juxtaposing corner dives with punk/hip-hop lounges and Those Who Tote MacBooks. Further out, Northeast spreads her fingers into distinct regions such as Georgia Ave, where middle-class blacks gossip in old-school diners and wi-fi-blasting pan-African cafés. Around Upshur St, once back of DC's beyond for transient types, the area becomes Far Northeast: residential, relaxed and increasingly peppered with bars that blend gritty hip and cozy camaraderie, a fellowship born from the sense that this is Washington's urban frontier.

COLUMBIA HEIGHTS & NORTHEAST

SEE

- Basilica of the National Shrine of the Immaculate Conception 1 F3
- Mt Pleasant Street 2 A3

EAT

- Don Juan Restaurant 3 A3
- Dos Gringos – A Mt Pleasant Café 4 A3
- Hitching Post 5 D1
- Sankofa Café 6 C4
- Sweet Mango Café 7 C2
- W Domku 8 C1

DRINK

- Looking Glass Lounge ...9 C2
- Raven 10 B3
- Red Derby 11 B2
- Tonic 12 B3

PLAY

- Wonderland 13 C3

Upper Northeast DC
Columbia Heights
Adams Morgan
Catholic University of America
Theological College
Trinity College
Children's National Medical Center
Howard University
Banneker Recreation Center
McMillan Park
McMillan Reservoir
Glenwood Cemetery
Piney Creek Park
Piney Branch
Georgia Ave–Petworth
To Franciscan Monastery (1.6mi)
To United States National Arboretum (3.7mi)
See Adams Morgan Map p105
See U Street & Shaw Map p81
0 200 m
0 0.1 miles
Blagden Ave NW
17th St NW
16th St NW
Arkansas Ave NW
14th St NW
13th St NW
Kansas Ave NW
Georgia Ave NW
New Hampshire Ave NW
Upshur St NW
Scale Gate Rd NW
Scale Gate Rd NE
Harwood Rd
Arnold Dr
Pershing Dr
N Capitol St
Michigan Ave NE
Michigan Ave NW
4th St NE
Spring Rd NW
Piney Branch Parkway NW
Parkwood Pl NW
10th St NW
Rock Creek NW
Quebec Pl NW
Princeton Pl NW
Otis Pl NW
Newton Pl NW
Park Rd NW
Morton St NW
Meridian Pl NW
Newton St NW
Monroe St NW
Mt Pleasant St NW
Lamont St NW
Kilbourne Pl NW
Kenyon St NW
Irving St NW
Hobart St NW
Harvard St NW
Quarry Rd NW
19th St NW
Hiatt Pl NW
15th St NW
Columbia Rd NW
Hobart Pl NW
Gresham St NW
Girard St NW
Fairmont St NW
Euclid St NW
Sherman Ave NW
6th St NW
4th St NW
1st St NW
Douglas St NW
Girard St NE
Franklin St NE
Lincoln Rd NE
Evarts St NE
Lanier Pl NW
Fuller St NW

SEE

BASILICA OF THE NATIONAL SHRINE OF THE IMMACULATE CONCEPTION

202-526-8400; www.nationalshrine.org; 400 Michigan Ave NE; 8:30am-7pm Apr-Oct, to 5pm Nov-Mar; M Brookland-CUA

The largest Catholic house of worship in North America is an enormous, impressive, but somehow unimposing edifice, more Byzantine than Vatican in its aesthetic. Outlaid with some 75,000 sq ft of mosaic work and a crypt modeled after early Christian catacombs, the (literal) crowning glory is a dome that could have been lifted off the Hagia Sophia in Istanbul.

FRANCISCAN MONASTERY

202-526-6800; www.myfranciscan.org; 1400 Quincy St NE; 9am-4pm

This honey-colored compound of ol' Assisi's order leaps out like an unexpected religious slap from the surrounding parkland and residential row houses. As a house of worship it's pretty but not particularly unique; more interesting are the carefully maintained grounds, threaded with walkways leading past 44 acres of serene gardens and unintentionally tacky re-creations of Holy Land sacred sites. You'll need to cab or drive out here.

MT PLEASANT STREET

www.mtpleasantdc.org; Mt Pleasant St NE; M Columbia Heights

There's no consensus as to why so many immigrants in the metro area are Central American as opposed to Mexican, but what can be confirmed is Mt Pleasant St is the *corazón* (heart) of DC's Latino, largely Salvadoran community. Every few businesses advertise money transfers to San Salvador, or sell cheap, delicious *pupusas* (Salvadoran baked turnovers stuffed with cheese and pork, or both) – try **Pupuseria San Miguel** (3110 Mt Pleasant St). Look out for the 7-Eleven, popularly known as 'El Seven,' on the corner of Kenyon St NW; the storefront is a popular informal hangout.

UNITED STATES NATIONAL ARBORETUM

202-245-2726; www.usna.usda.gov; 3501 New York Ave NE; admission free, tram tour adult/child/student $4/2/3; 8am-5pm

The best things in life require a little effort. In this case, you need wheels to reach the greatest green space in Washington, almost 450 acres of meadowland, sylvan theaters, and a pastoral setting that feels somewhere between bucolic Americana countryside and a Romantic artist's conception of classical Greek landscapes.

John K Groth

Marketing Director, Donatelli Development, manager of marketing, advertising and events for DC apartment and condo developments

Where do you think DC's next neighborhood for affordable food, fun etc is going to be? Petworth [in Northeast] is receiving buzz lately. New luxury buildings are opening, along with dozens of restaurants and bars, like the established W Domku (p101) and the recently opened Looking Glass Lounge (p102). **Why do you live in Columbia Heights?** The neighborhood is up-and-coming, but a little slower paced than U St, where I used to live. I love the niche places like Wonderland Ballroom (p103), Red Derby (p103) and Tonic (p103). The Raven (p102) might be the best dive bar in the city. **Why do you think people should live in, not just visit, DC?** DC is too culturally diverse to take in and appreciate without immersing yourself in things beyond Georgetown and the monuments.

The golden altar at the impressive Basilica of the National Shrine of the Immaculate Conception (p98)

EAT

DON JUAN RESTAURANT

Latin American $

☎ 202-667-0010; 1600 Lamont St NW; 9am-2am; M Columbia Heights

Don Juan's is the keystone of the Mt Pleasant St arch (along with nearby Best Way Groceries, one of DC's biggest Latino supermarkets). While it may not serve the best Latin American food in the city, the chow is still good (try the black bean soup for a pleasant easy-on-a-conservative-stomach breakfast). More importantly, it's a bedrock for local Central Americans, where they meet, greet, eat and gossip.

DOS GRINGOS – A MT PLEASANT CAFÉ

Latin American $

☎ 202-462-1159; www.dosgringoscafe.com; 3116 Mt Pleasant St NW; 7:30am-8pm Tue-Thu, to 9pm Fri, 9am-9pm Sat, 9am-4pm Sun; M Columbia Heights

You gotta chuckle at both the self deprecation and *cajones* of putting this, well, gringo-owned café in the middle of Mt Pleasant and naming it as such. Not that anyone resents Dos Gringos' presence; Latinos and Anglos alike line up to order off a bilingual menu that includes fresh veg burritos, cheap cups of coffee, curry chicken salads and portobello sandwiches served in an Ikea-chic interior.

HITCHING POST *Soul* $

202-726-1511; 200 Upshur St NW; 10:30am-10pm Tue-Sat; M Georgia Ave-Petworth

'This is East Coast jazz,' says the owner behind the counter. 'No one listens to this anymore.' Another song comes up; the Drifters. Really? The Drifters and jazz in a diner so neighborly it should put on a cardigan and loafers when it comes inside? Let's try the fried chicken…which, ohmigod, is seriously like a whole, freaking fried chicken. Served with *two* sides. And another man comes in and the owner calls him by name and the customer asks, 'This the Chi-Lites?,' and we know we're in love.

SANKOFA CAFÉ *Vegetarian* $

202-332-1084; 2714 Georgia Ave NW; 10:30am-10pm Tue-Sat; M Columbia Heights

Good for your soul and your body, Sankofa is basically a black intellectual café expounding the old-school Pan-African ideal. In the 21st century it still fronts an excellent African/African American–themed bookstore and video place, but don't miss the sandwiches, salads and wraps; the latter constitute some of the best vegan fare in town. We're all about the 'Gaston Kabore' – garlic hummus, honey Dijon, olives etc served in an excellent tortilla.

SWEET MANGO CAFÉ *Caribbean* $

202-726-6246; www.sweetmangocafe.com; 3701 New Hampshire Ave NW; 11am-10pm Mon-Wed, to 11pm Thu, to midnight Fri & Sat, to 8pm Sun; M Georgia Ave-Petworth

Sweet Mango is a popular lunch stop for office workers and West Indian immigrants alike, who crowd in for very fine executions of standards like ox-tail, jerk chicken on rice and beans, and, of course, plantains. The rooftop terrace, the aforementioned food and a cold drink pretty much make for a perfect start to a hot and humid DC summer's eve.

W DOMKU *European* $$

202-722-7475; www.domkucafe.com; 821 Upshur St NW; 5-11pm Tue & Wed, 10am-11pm Thu, to midnight Fri & Sat, to 10pm Sun; M Georgia Ave-Petworth

As unexpected as…well, a hip, artsy coffee shop in the middle of a very local strip of churches, funeral homes and Caribbean takeouts, Domku is a gem. The interior is like Ikea on good drugs, and the food is an intriguing execution of Polish, Norwegian and

DC A GO-GO

On any given night, you're likely to see a man set up plastic barrels and beat out a rhythm that grabs you by the guts and throws your booty to the wall. That's go-go, folks: DC's homegrown subset of, depending on who you ask, funk (if they're over 30) and hip-hop (if younger). Driven by heavy beats – timbales, bass, percussion of any type – it's a niche genre of dance music whose popularity is limited to DC (even Baltimoreans don't like it). When we say homegrown, we mean ghetto-born, and go-go's still outgrowing those rough roots; shootings in go-go clubs have led to their closure in much of town. But you can always catch DC's dance grooves at night on 93.9 FM and 95.5 FM, when Chuck Brown, Mambo Sauce, Rare Essence and other originals grace the airwaves.

Russian fare – 'gypsy sandwiches,' poached eggs topped with caviar, and pancakes baked on clouds dappled with lavender compote.

DRINK

LOOKING GLASS LOUNGE *Lounge*

☎ 202-722-7669; 3634 Georgia Ave NW; 5pm-1:30am Mon-Thu, to 2:30am Fri & Sat; M Georgia Ave-Petworth

Here's who you expect to find when you look through the Looking Glass: an old guy, one who's owned his chair at the bar for decades, in a broad-brimmed cap and clutching a highball of Jameson as if to prove it. And that guy is here. But drinking next to him is a crowd of 20- and 30-somethings who respect his presence, even as they crank the music under dark chandelier-ish lighting and commiserate in the beer garden out back.

RAVEN *Dive*

☎ 202-347-8411; 3125 Mt Pleasant Ave NW; noon-2am; M Columbia Heights

The best jukebox in Washington, a dark interior crammed with locals and lovers, neon lighting that casts you under a glow Edward

Bar camaraderie at ubercool Red Derby

Hopper should rightly paint and a tough but friendly bar staff are the ingredients in this shot, which, when slammed, hits you as DC's best dive by a mile.

RED DERBY *Lounge*

202-291-5000; www.redderby.com; 3718 14th St NW; 5pm-2am Mon-Thu, to 3am Fri, 11am-3am Sat & Sun; M Columbia Heights/Georgia Ave-Petworth

There's no sign – always a good sign – just the symbol of a red hat. Underneath that cap is a hipster-punk lounge where the 'tenders know the names, the sweet-potato fries soak up the beer ordered off an impressively long menu and – why yes, that is *The Princess Bride* – movies play on a projector screen. The lighting is blood red and sexy, natch; you can't help but look good under it.

TONIC *Lounge*

202-986-7661; 3155 Mt Pleasant St NW; 5pm-2am Sun-Thu, to 3am Fri & Sat; M Columbia Heights

A new genre is challenging DC's reputation for downtown-y, slick uberlounges and clubs. The response is low-key atmosphere and friendly service, but still enough raucous fun to give the party that bacchanalian edge by the time closing drinks get called. Tonic was one of the first exemplars of this revolution, and long may she wave her banner for all of the above.

PLAY

WONDERLAND *Live Music*

202-232-5263; www.thewonderlandballroom.com; 1101 Kenyon St NW; 5pm-2am; M Columbia Heights

There are standards. When we've had a long night, or when we need a good night out, whatever, we repair here. It's punk downstairs, hip-hop up, a beer garden where you smoke and make friends, and casual friendliness but with enough sexy to make you feel like dancing, drinking, devilry. Damn we love you.

>ADAMS MORGAN

The answer 'Adams Morgan' to the question 'Where are we going out tonight?' elicits two reactions in Washington: an excited shriek or a resigned sigh. As nightlife goes, many people consider this DC's version of that one part of your town – you know the one – where the just-of-age get too drunk too quickly.

That cliché does the Morgan a disservice. Nightlife came here on the heels of cheap rents and immigrant influxes, which makes this one of the best spots in town for the alliterative eats of Ethiopian and El Salvadoran. Vintage boutiques and indie record shops stand above West African and Brazilian cafés, leading to one of Adams Morgan's great nightlife questions: to *lingala* or *lambada?* Get past the silliness of the slicker bars and you'll find a marriage of ethnicities and entertainment that has kept this 'hood justifiably popular with the eat-drink-and-be-merry crowd for decades.

ADAMS MORGAN

👁 SEE
Malcolm X Park1 E3
Meridian House &
 International Center ...2 E3

🛍 SHOP
B&K Newsstand3 D3
Brass Knob4 D3
Crooked Beat Records ...5 D3
Meeps & Aunt Neensie's
 Vintage Clothing6 D4

Shake Your Booty7 D3
Skynear & Co8 D3

🍴 EAT
Bardia's9 D3
Meskerem10 C2
Mixtec11 D2
Pasta Mia12 D2
Tryst13 D2

🍸 DRINK
Dan's Café14 D3
Madam's Organ15 D2
Reef16 C2

⭐ PLAY
Chief Ike's
 Mambo Room17 D1
Ghana Café18 D2

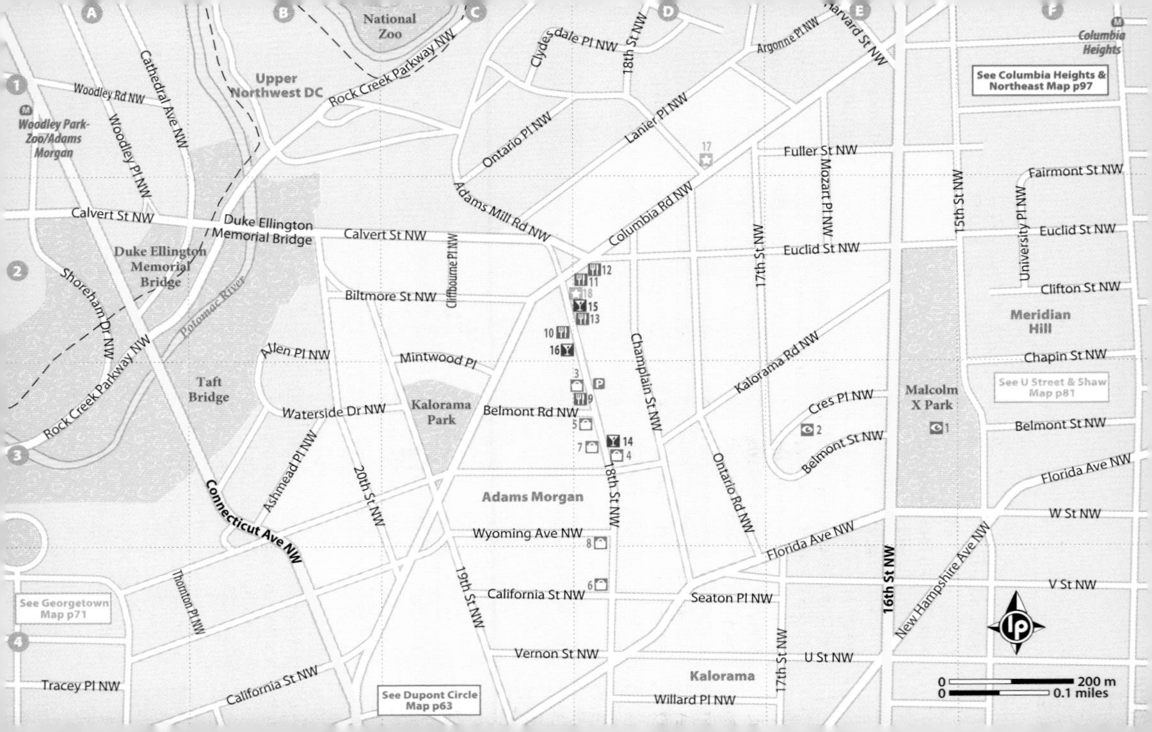

National Zoo
Upper Northwest DC
Woodley Park-Zoo/Adams Morgan
Columbia Heights
See Columbia Heights & Northeast Map p97
Woodley Rd NW
Cathedral Ave NW
Woodley Pl NW
Rock Creek Parkway NW
Clydesdale Pl NW
18th St NW
Argonne Pl NW
Harvard St NW
Lanier Pl NW
Ontario Pl NW
Adams Mill Rd NW
Columbia Rd NW
Fuller St NW
Mozart Pl NW
Fairmont St NW
15th St NW
University Pl NW
Euclid St NW
Calvert St NW
Duke Ellington Memorial Bridge
Cliffbourne Pl NW
17th St NW
Clifton St NW
Meridian Hill
Shoreham Dr NW
Potomac River
Biltmore St NW
Allen Pl NW
Mintwood Pl
Kalorama Rd NW
Champlain St NW
Chapin St NW
Taft Bridge
Kalorama Park
Belmont Rd NW
Waterside Dr NW
Cres Pl NW
Malcolm X Park
See U Street & Shaw Map p81
Belmont St NW
Ashmead Pl NW
20th St NW
Ontario Rd NW
Florida Ave NW
Connecticut Ave NW
Adams Morgan
Wyoming Ave NW
W St NW
16th St NW
New Hampshire Ave NW
19th St NW
California St NW
Seaton Pl NW
V St NW
Thornton Pl NW
See Georgetown Map p71
Vernon St NW
U St NW
Kalorama
Tracey Pl NW
See Dupont Circle Map p63
Willard Pl NW
0 200 m
0 0.1 miles
A
B
C
D
E
F
1
2
3
4

SEE

MALCOLM X PARK

btwn W, 15th, 16th & Euclid Sts NW; M U Street-Cardozo

This is frankly an incredible bit of green space (known to the uninitiated as Meridian Park) that gets short shrift in the list of America's great urban parks. What makes it special is the way the park emphasizes its distinctive geography. Lying on the fall line between the upland Piedmont Plateau and flat Atlantic Coastal Plain, the grounds are terraced like hanging gardens replete with waterfalls, sandstone terraces and assorted embellishments that feel almost Tuscan.

MERIDIAN HOUSE & INTERNATIONAL CENTER

☎ 202-667-6800; www.meridian.org; 1630 Crescent Pl NW; admission free; 2-5pm Wed-Sun; M U Street-Cardozo

People who've lived here for years haven't heard of Meridian House, which isn't surprising: this impressive mansion springs out of nowhere, looking like the HQ for some world-dominating secret society. In fact, it's an education and hospitality center for DC's international community; the interior grounds are as impressive as the building's exterior.

SHOP

B&K NEWSSTAND

Head Shop/Newsstand

☎ 202-628-8306; 2414 18th St NW; 9am-9pm; M U Street-Cardozo

No one asks for the *New York Times*, because B&K is really a head (pipe) shop, one of the most famed among the city's stoner set. All glassware is, of course, to be used for tobacco smoking. Beyond all the pipes and bongs is an almost clichéd array of Bob Marley paraphernalia along with other Amsterdam-esque accoutrements.

GETTING TO THE PARTY

A bit annoyingly, one of the city's most popular strips of food and nightlife – 18th St NW between U and Euclid Sts – is not directly Metro accessible. It's not hard to reach, though. From the Woodley Park-Zoo/Adams Morgan Metro station (Red Line), it's a 20-minute walk across the Duke Ellington Bridge into Adams Morgan proper, and from U Street-Cardozo Metro (Green Line) it takes roughly the same time walking up U St. Both walks are safe, the former running over scenic parkland, the latter ambling through more restaurants and bars. The U Link bus traditionally connected the above two stations via 18th St, but as of press time plans seemed confirmed to link Adams Morgan to the DC Circulator route (which runs all the way to K St) for $1.

BRASS KNOB *Vintage*

☎ 202-332-3370; www.brassknob.com; 2311 18th St NW; 🕒 10:30am-6pm Mon-Sat, noon-5pm Sun; Ⓜ Woodley Park-Zoo/Adams Morgan

The title says the store's specialty – any doorknob you've ever wanted – but there are all sorts of culled antiquities of pretty much any material but wood for sale: bronze, copper, glass, concrete. If you need to accent your crib like the interior of the best old DC row houses, look no further.

CROOKED BEAT RECORDS *Music*

☎ 202-483-2328; 2318 18th St NW; 🕒 2-9pm Mon, noon-9pm Tue & Wed, noon-10pm Thu-Sat, noon-7pm Sun; Ⓜ Woodley Park-Zoo/Adams Morgan

Go underground to enter this excellent record shop, the sort of place that in the '90s could have been its own movie about a bunch of aimless 20-somethings finding love amid stacks of indie, hip-hop and vinyl…you get the idea. Trust us; it's a cool music shop, and to their enormous credit, the folks behind the counter are eminently down to earth.

MEEPS & AUNT NEENSIE'S VINTAGE CLOTHING *Vintage*

☎ 202-265-6546; www.meepsdc.com; 2104 18th St NW; 🕒 noon-7pm Mon-Sat, to 5pm Sun; Ⓜ U Street-Cardozo

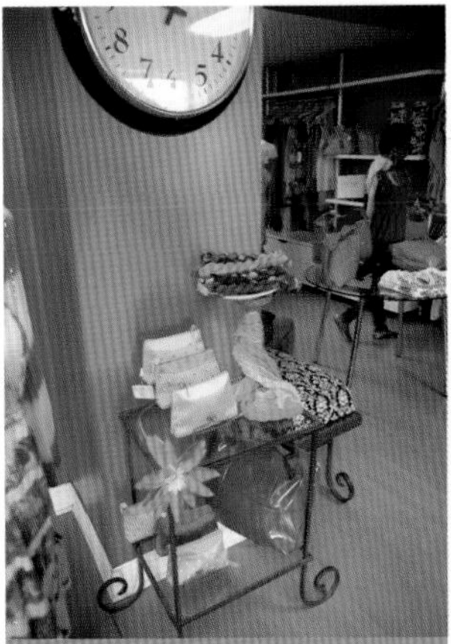

Get bootiful like Beyoncé at Shake Your Booty

There's this girl you know: extremely stylish and never seems to have a brand name on her body. Now, picture her wardrobe. Now enter, pick what you like off the racks, *et voila:* there's Meeps mapped out for you.

SHAKE YOUR BOOTY *Clothing*

☎ 202-518-8205; 2439 18th St NW; 🕒 noon-8pm Mon-Fri, to 9pm Sat, to 6pm Sun; Ⓜ U Street-Cardozo

This pretty boutique cutes up its appreciative audience of fashionistas with hip outfits that feel as cool as Lucite and as glam as a bit of bling, which is kind of the point. A lot of indie shops in town are

Kenny Carroll

Executive Director of DC WritersCorps and literature teacher at Duke Ellington High School for the Arts

It's been said Washington is too divided for there to ever be a great DC novel. It's DC's divisions that ultimately make it a fertile ground for great novels. Great is subjective and usually measured decades from the novel's epicenter, but some that I think could eventually be considered: Marita Golden's *A Long Distance Life, Edge of Heaven,* and *After*; Percival Everett's *Erasure*; Stephen Carter's *Emperor of Ocean Park*; and Patricia Browning Griffith's *Supporting the Sky*. **Where would you take a visitor who wanted to look past the Mall?** I'd take them to the African American Civil War Museum (p82) or the Anacostia Museum (p43). I'd have them check out the city's two most beautiful vistas: Malcolm X Park (p106) and the overlook at Our Lady of Perpetual Help (1600 Morris Rd SE). Of course, I'd take them to U St for self-absorbed poetry readings, hip-hop performances and a half smoke from Ben's Chili Bowl (p84).

a bit monochrome, but Booty is, perhaps appropriately, less Belle and Sebastian, more Beyoncé.

SKYNEAR & CO *Homewares*

202-797-7160; 2122 18th St NW; 11am-7pm Mon-Sat, noon-6pm Sun; M U Street-Cardozo

How much hip can fit over several floors of fab, and what is hip anyways? A bronze candelabra patina-ed with history bordering on romance? Barack Obama T-shirts where the president's face is assembled from rhinestones? How about Japanese-style removable room partitions? Whatever: it's all for sale in Skynear.

EAT

Adams Morgan isn't just where everyone seems to party; it's also where everyone seems to get the food that soaks up the party. Huge slices of pizza are a traditional DC post-bar snack; they're sold everywhere around here and are uniformly greasy and delicious when drunk. Or try Julia's empanadas at **Julia's Empanadas** (1001 18th St); we recommend the chorizo.

BARDIA'S *Southern* $$

202-234-0420; 2412 18th St NW; 10am-10pm; M U Street-Cardozo

We have it on good authority (the stoners stumbling out of

Let's make a Tryst (p111) to sink some 'Schlager at Adams Morgan's Madam's Organ (p111)

B&K Newsstand; see p106) that this New Orleans–style café is the best cure for munchies in town. But that stereotype's a disservice. Bardia's food – the po' boys, the breakfasts and especially the beignets – is fantastic whatever your mental state.

MESKEREM *African* $$

☎ 202-462-4100; 2434 18th St NW; 🕑 noon-midnight Sun-Fri, to 1am Sat; Ⓜ Woodley Park/Adams Morgan

Washington is full of Ethiopian restaurants, but Meskerem still holds the crown as far as we're concerned. It's the just-seared lamb served in spicy sauce, the *wat* (stew) scooped with spongy *injera* (pancakelike bread) and the vegetables, all deliciously spiced, not hot but rich, complex and savory. This is remarkably easy food for the most conservative palette, best washed down with some imported honey wine.

MIXTEC *Mexican* $

☎ 202-332-1011; 1792 Columbia Rd NW; 🕑 10am-10pm Sun-Thu, to 11pm Fri & Sat; Ⓜ Woodley Park/Adams Morgan

Our favorite Mexican diner does an excellent line in huevos rancheros and moles (the chocolate version on chicken is particularly divine), and the best hot chocolate – kinda bittersweet and pretty much made of silk – in town. It's also definitely

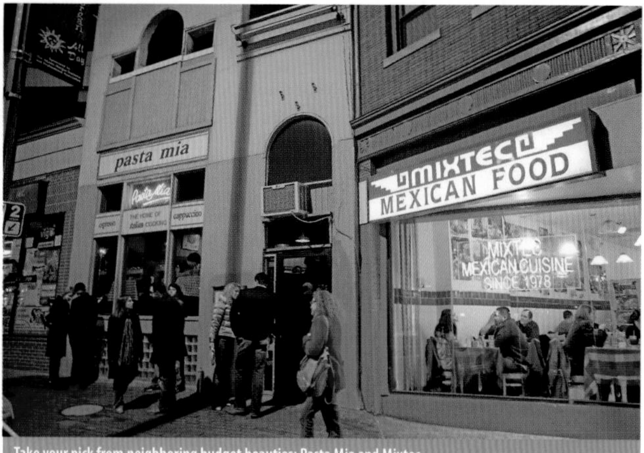

Take your pick from neighboring budget beauties: Pasta Mia and Mixtec

one of the best food for money ratios in town; you're almost guaranteed to bust your gut for less than $10.

PASTA MIA *European* $

☎ 202-328-9114; 1790 Columbia Rd NW; 5-10pm Mon-Sat; M Woodley Park/Adams Morgan

Long lines, stiff waitstaff, crowded conditions, perfect pasta. This is the price of good, cheap Italian, friends. But that's OK – sip your red, twirl one of 20 or so types of flour/semolina/gram perfection and try not to break into operatic praise. It gets crowded inside, so this may not be the best place for romantic candlelight and Chianti, although it is grand for big groups and gregariousness.

TRYST *American* $

☎ 202-232-5500; www.trystdc.com; 2459 18th St NW; 6:30-2am Mon-Thu, to 3am Fri & Sat, 8am-12:30am Sun; M Woodley Park/Adams Morgan

'So-and-so is Trysting' seems to be a perennial Facebook status/Twitter update in DC, which automatically tells you what to expect here: good coffee, good sandwiches, lots of Macs (no wi-fi on weekends, though). Come nightfall, baristas become bartenders, and rather good ones too.

DRINK

DAN'S CAFÉ *Dive*

☎ 202-265-9241; 2315 18th St NW; from 7:30pm Sun-Thu; M U Street-Cardozo

Dan's dive is all the more grotty for its location: smack in the middle of the 18th St skimpy skirt parade. Inside this barely signed bar is dim lighting, old locals, J Crew–looking types slumming it, and flasks of whiskey, coke and a bucket of ice on sale for under $12(!).

MADAM'S ORGAN *Live Music*

☎ 202-667-5370; www.madamsorgan.com; 2461 18th St NW; to 2am; M Woodley Park/Adams Morgan

The ol' Organ is a standard, a wood-and-dust-and-shots-of-'Schlager kind of place where the music is American – jazz, blues and bluegrass – and, when the shows get going, the ambience just shy of (and occasionally nudging into) sheer apocalyptic chaos.

REEF *Lounge*

☎ 202-464-4540; 2446 18th St NW; to 2am; M Woodley Park/Adams Morgan

We mainly come to Reef for the roof, which is heavenly on hot capital nights, but somehow, everyone always ends up in the aquarium-studded main lounge.

WORTH THE TRIP

West of Rock Creek Park and above Calvert St is **Upper Northwest, DC**, a green and good stretch of livability that extends in an upper-left diagonal toward Maryland. These are literally DC's houses on the hill (well, series of hills), a spiderweb of tree-lined boulevards, nice restaurants, a Sith Lord–crowned cathedral and the **National Zoo** (☎ 202-673-4800; http://nationalzoo.si.edu; 3001 Connecticut Ave NW; admission free; 🕑 6am-8pm Apr-Oct, to 6pm Nov-Mar; Ⓜ Woodley Park-Zoo/Adams Morgan). Now entering its 120th year of existence, the zoo celebrates a birthday attended by some controversy, hope (two words: giant pandas) and cautious optimism exemplified by the birth of a lowland gorilla. Still one of the best zoos around, the National gently sprawls over 163 acres cut through by a mini-Amazon, the interactive Think Tank and the excellent Asia Trail, which winds around aforementioned pandas, clouded leopards and red pandas.

Nearby is **Rock Creek Park** (☎ 202-895-6070; www.nps.gov/rocr; Ⓜ Cleveland Park or Woodley Park-Zoo/Adams Morgan), which, at more than 1700 acres, is twice the size of Central Park (and feels loads wilder). You can feel utterly isolated from the city here (sometimes too isolated; the park can be dangerous after dark), but beyond wilderness escapism, make sure you pop into the local planetarium and see the art in the next-door Rock Creek Gallery.

Like his predecessors, the day after inauguration Barack Obama attended a multifaith service at the **National Cathedral** (☎ 202-537-6200; www.nationalcathedral.org; Massachusetts & Wisconsin Ave NW; 🕑 10am-4:30pm; Ⓜ Tenleytown), a neo-Gothic assertion of America's talent for religious architecture and blending – while technically Episcopal, the cathedral also hosts Muslim, Jewish, Buddhist and Baha'i worshippers. Be on the lookout for quirky gargoyles, including one of Darth Vader's helmeted head.

If you need a quick cheap bite, the pizza at **Vace's Deli** (☎ 202-363-1999; 3315 Connecticut Ave NW; 🕑 9am-9pm Mon-Fri, to 8pm Sat, 10:30am-5pm Sun) is divine. In the same tomato-sauce vein, **Comet Ping Pong** (☎ 202-364-0404; www.cometpingpong.com; 5037 Connecticut Ave NW; 🕑 5-9:30pm Mon-Thu, to 10:30pm Fri, 11am-10:30pm Sat, to 8pm Sun; Ⓜ Van Ness-UDC) satisfies your deepest nostalgias. A round of ping pong in the back is perfectly complemented by the 'smoky' – smoked bacon, gouda and mushrooms (drool). For more of a splurge, pop into **Palena** (☎ 202-537-9250; www.palenarestaurant.com; 3529 Connecticut Ave NW; 🕑 5:30-10pm Tue-Sat; Ⓜ Cleveland Park) and get ready for a culinary ride into innovative gastro-orgasm land. The menu defies our conventions, deliciously: Swiss chard served in ink ravioli, sturgeon wrapped in pancetta, and pheasant consommé. The interior is warm but oddly modern in its crafted rusticity; to see or eat any of the above, book early.

Before you leave this 'hood, get your read on in **Politics & Prose** (☎ 202-364-1919; www.politics-prose.com; 5015 Connecticut Ave NW; 🕑 9am-10pm Mon-Sat, 10am-8pm Sun; Ⓜ Van Ness-UDC). One of Washington's best bookstores offers quiet spaces for browsing a deep array of titles, free wi-fi throughout, a café, quiet and all the other ingredients required for that perfect, latte-laced intellectual bouillabaisse.

It's usually packed with the hot and the hot-to-trot, so sink a pint and make a friend next to the fishies.

PLAY

CHIEF IKE'S MAMBO ROOM *Lounge*

☎ 202-332-2211; 1725 Columbia Rd NW; 9pm-2am; M Woodley Park/Adams Morgan

What we love about Ike's is how it's a place to get a good Latin groove going…while surrounded by leering *Evil Dead*–esque murals of psychedelic voodoo zombies and assorted other undead. There are punk and hip-hop clubs upstairs if you tire of monster-movie mambo.

GHANA CAFÉ *Lounge*

☎ 202-387-3845; 2465 18th St NW; 9pm-2am; M Woodley Park/Adams Morgan

You thought you could move your ass, but the butts here shake your booty into sorry submission. Come see DC's West African expats get their weekend going, and be prepared for sore but happy hips the next morning.

>SNAPSHOTS

Rain slanting over the Capitol dome; activists arguing policy in a pub; Redskins jerseys and chili half smokes on a fall day; jazz reverberating across Logan Circle in summer. These are just some of the indelible images of Washington – here's where to find more.

Smile for George! The Mall (p34), Washington Monument (p41) and admirers

ACCOMMODATIONS

The Washington sleeping scene has always been pretty good. Dusting the top end of the scale are some of the city's classic accommodations, monuments of Victorian and jazz-era opulence that remain some of our favorite spots for a capital crash. Exemplars include the **Hay-Adams** (www.hayadams.com), **St Regis** (www.stregis.com), the **Melrose** (www.melrosehotel.com) and the **Morrison Clark** (www.morrisonclark.com), all of which have the bells and whistles you'd expect from any high-end hotel, along with a scope of history other American cities have a hard time matching: when rooms are called the 'Roosevelt suite' here, it's because Teddy actually slept there.

Over the past two decades folks in need of a Washington bed have become more demanding and (ostensibly) more hip. As a result, new digs have a bit of edge, including boutique sleeps such as the **Rouge** (www.rougehotel.com), the **Helix** (www.hotelhelix.com) and to a lesser extent, the **Palomar** (www.hotelpalomar-dc.com), all located in the Dupont Circle–U St–Adams Morgan triangle of fun, and all reasonably midrange in price to boot.

If you're looking for character and don't mind if said character is redolent of Old Washington (but in a sip-sherry-at-noon, not mothballs-in-your-shoes kind of way), B&Bs may be your best bet. Generally set in elegant old row houses, they may not compete with the big boys in the amenities or leg-room stakes, but they're atmospheric as hell and in shoulder and off seasons you can often score a room for under $100. The following are located around Dupont Circle and Adams Morgan. Try the inns of the **Dupont Collection** (www.thedupontcollection.com), **Adams Inn** (www.adamsinn.com), **Kalorama Guest House** (www.kaloramaguesthouse.com) and **Dupont at the Circle** (www.dupontatthecircle.com).

For something in between all of the places previously listed – classic but not too expensive, a sense of history without the unasked-for intimacy of a B&B – lots of hotels here manage to combine large-scale space and efficient high occupancy with embellishments of another age, be it deco at the **Windsor** (www.windsor-inn-dc.com), Tudor at the **Tabard** (www.tabardinn.com) or colonial at **George Washington University Inn** (www.gwuinn.com).

We can't finish without mentioning two of DC's greatest (and priciest) hotels: the **Mansion on O Street** (www.omansion.com) in Dupont Circle, a sort of private club-cum-surrealist temple to refined excess, and the beaux arts **Willard** (www.washington.intercontinental.com) near the White House, where Ulysses Grant coined the term 'lobbyist' and MLK wrote 'I Have a Dream.'

WEB RESOURCES

You can find unbiased reviews and book online at Hotels & Hostels on lonelyplanet.com. Other centralized accommodation sites for DC are www.washingtondchotels.com, www.thedistrict.com and www.bedandbreakfastdc.com.

PLUSH & POSH

- > Willard (www.washington.intercontinental.com)
- > Jefferson Hotel (www.thejeffersonwashingtondc.com)
- > Hotel Monaco (www.monaco-dc.com)
- > Hay-Adams (www.hayadams.com)
- > St Regis (www.stregis.com)

THE WILD ONES

- > Helix (www.hotelhelix.com)
- > Rouge (www.rougehotel.com)
- > Brickskeller Inn (www.lovethebeer.com/brickskeller-inn.html)
- > Hotel Palomar (www.hotelpalomar-dc.com)
- > Mansion on O Street (www.omansion.com)

BEST B&B BETS

- > Dupont Collection (www.thedupontcollection.com)
- > Swan House (www.swanhouse.com)
- > Woodley Park Guest House (www.woodleyparkguesthouse.com)
- > Dupont at the Circle (www.dupontatthecircle.com)
- > Taft Bridge Inn (www.taftbridgeinn.com)

CHEAP & CHEERFUL

- > Washington International Student Center (www.dchostel.com)
- > Kalorama Guest House (www.kaloramaguesthouse.com)
- > Hilltop Hostel (www.hosteldc.com)
- > Adam's Inn (www.adamsinn.com)
- > Hostelling International – Washington DC (www.hiwashingtondc.org)

MONUMENTS & MUSEUMS

Thomas Jefferson, paradox that he was (slave-owning proponent of liberty and freedom), captured the dichotomies and eccentricities of his nation when he insisted on a 'universal' theory of knowledge, the idea that absorbing all expression from every corner of the globe was nothing less than humankind's ultimate goal. A difficult one, too, but an ambition oft attempted by city fathers of the capital he helped found: bringing the collected intellectual and aesthetic accomplishments of humanity to one spot, for the perusal of anyone interested in what the human race has been up to.

The thing is, it kinda worked. Washington, DC may quite possibly have the best concentration of monumental architecture and museums in the world – and the majority of it is free. But let's mention the stuff you pay for first so it doesn't get deluged by all the gratis goodness. To whit: the Corcoran Gallery (p90), International Spy Museum (p56) and Newseum (p39) all charge for entry, but the latter two institutions will keep your kids happy, while the former is a feast of fine arts that we'd confidently compare to even London and Paris.

But then…there's the Smithsonian. Oh sweet Smithsonian – was ever an eccentric antimonarchist Englishman's endowment better spent (see p145)? There just isn't a bad Smithsonian museum – trust us, we've looked. And while we'd love it (actually, dammit, we insist) if the institution were better funded, we have to admit that lack of cash has brought a volunteer staff out of the woodwork that performs nothing short of educational miracles when it comes to showing you around the cultural treasures our nation has amassed. That said, the whole universal knowledge concept is best realized in the Library of Congress (p46), a building dedicated to the cause of collecting every written record ever and making it available to you.

Washington's monuments evoke mixed reactions. They can be ubiquitous to the point that they lose their power; even uberpatriots will often admit to feeling a little weary of this or that stone statue to such and such an obscure figure, especially those paragons of mediocrity who kissed the right butts at the right time (George Meade could have ended the Civil War two years early if he'd got off his butt at Gettysburg, and he gets a statue that makes you think he was the Second Coming).

This sort of silliness is unavoidable – what and who we choose to enshrine as a nation will always be a controversial decision. But in a way, that's the beauty of the monuments. As you peruse them, you see what Americans considered important throughout time – some second-rate Civil War general in the 1890s, and African American veterans of the same conflict in the 1990s. And for every forgettable bearded guy on a horse is an Iwo Jima memorial (p76) or execution of an era in stone (see the FDR memorial, p36) engraved into the capital landscape. Because so many American victories were as much about winning internal rights as defeating external opponents, there are moments when the monuments aren't so much arrogant, or even majestic, but inspiring. In your visit to Washington, you have the opportunity to pass what you don't care for and reflect at those spots that make you feel, not more American, but more likely to ponder what being American is. Even if you're not one.

BEST PERMANENT MUSEUM EXHIBITIONS

- > Japanese silk scrolls, Freer and Sackler Gallery (p36)
- > Main exhibition, United States Holocaust Memorial Museum (p40)
- > Folk art galleries, Smithsonian American Art Museum (p56)
- > The dinosaurs, Smithsonian's National Museum of Natural History (p39)
- > First floor, National Portrait Gallery (p56)

BEST SPOTS FOR FEELING AS AMERICAN AS APPLE PIE

- > Lincoln Memorial (p37)
- > The Capitol (p43)
- > The White House (p91)
- > National Archives (p38)
- > Vietnam Veterans Memorial (p40)

Left The imposing facade of Washington's largest private museum: the Corcoran Gallery of Art (p90)

ARCHITECTURE

Most savvy visitors to the capital pick up on the income gap as Washington's most glaring dichotomy, and they're making a pretty accurate observation in the process. But there's another contradiction looming over DC, obvious and awesome in its scope.

Great buildings versus godawful ones.

Seriously. How could a city that has given us neoclassical gems such as the Library of Congress (p46), Lincoln Memorial (p37), National Archives (p38) and the Capitol itself (p43) also produce marbled monstrosities like the IRS Building? How could the powerful innovation of the Vietnam Veterans Memorial (p40) and east wing of the National Gallery of Art (p38) get plopped so close to the boxy National Air & Space Museum (p37) or (shudder) the steel-and-concrete Hoover Building, headquarters of the FBI?

All of the above aside, here's the main thing to remember when experiencing Washington as a city of buildings: DC may possess the greatest concentration of architectural styles for a city of its size in the entire world. The capital has always felt the need to prove itself: as center of the ideal republic, to Europe, to the world, and every so often, to its citizens.

So: we've got the neoclassical sweep of buildings that evokes the ancient Greek and Roman republics lining the National Mall (p34). The extravagant, turn-of-the-century optimism embodied by the beaux arts movement, best realized in Union Station (p48) and the Historical Society of Washington, DC (p56), formerly the city library. The humble impact of the Federal style, which evokes the elegance of the best European architecture overlaid with an emphasis on modesty and understatement – wander through Georgetown (p72) or visit the Octagon Museum (p90) and St John's Church (p91) to see what we're driving at. And then there's the cutting edge of contemporary design, the effort to set DC ahead of the building pack. Sometimes, the effort fails (Hoover Building!), but sometimes, as evidenced by the sinuous, warm curves of the National Museum of the American Indian (p39), our newest buildings become our city's greatest resource.

OUR FAVORITE FEDERAL-STYLE ICONS

- > Old Stone House (p73)
- > Octagon Museum (p90)
- > Capitol Hill row houses (p42)
- > Georgetown mansions (p70)
- > Phillips Collection (p64)

MODERN MARVELS

- > Hirshhorn Museum & Sculpture Garden (p36)
- > Interior, United States Holocaust Memorial Museum (p40)
- > East wing of the National Gallery of Art (p38)
- > Central courtyard, Smithsonian American Art Museum (p56)
- > National Museum of the American Indian (p39)

Above Washington, DC in the 21st century or ancient Greek republic? The Lincoln Memorial (p37) anchoring the Mall's west end

FOOD

Washington is a great city for food; even better, it lacks foodies. By that we don't mean people who appreciate food, rather the obsessed who patter on as though food was the only yardstick worth measuring a town by – well, we are trying to run a country here, guys.

But Washingtonians do like to eat. Locals, who live at the fault line of Northeast ethnic enclaves and Southern soul, are naturals at mixing. If you're from down the block, you're lucky, because you've had the best *wat* (Ethiopian stew; p110) this side of Addis Ababa. You knew you had to cross the border to northern Virginia for *pho* (Vietnamese noodle soup; p76) and to Maryland for crab cakes. You figured out lake trout never swam near a lake, but tastes great anyways (especially with greens and mac 'n' cheese), and that nothing soaks up the beer like a half smoke from Ben's (p84).

But there's fabulous, multistarred top-end dining here too, which was initially attracted by all the wealthy bigwigs who didn't care much about where they ate, as long as it was expensive and classy. The result was a dining scene that was pretentious and not at the same time – top-class chefs moved into town, but their clientele wasn't all that discerning. The balance of this equation was better than you may think: all that talent had free range to play and the wonderful Chesapeake tidewater to draw off, as sourcing ingredients became more of a local phenomenon. In between all the patrician posturing, a culinary explosion occurred.

Actually, there's another way of putting this: while we don't want to harp on about race and class, those are the major identifiers in this town. In short, DC has become more of a middle-class city over the past two decades, and the result has been fewer corner spots, more midrange dining options and a conscious effort by high-end restaurants to appeal to a lower price point. All social commentary aside, this transformation has raised the profile of Washington's once sneered-at food scene, and as the middle class itself becomes more multihued, more folks are getting seats at Washington's table (OK, there's some commentary).

BEST ETHNIC EATS

> Bistrot du Coin (French, p66)
> Mitsitam Café (Native American, p41)
> Meskerem (Ethiopian, p110)
> Judy's (Salvadoran, p85)
> Burma (Burmese, p58)

BEST UPSCALE EATERIES

> Minibar at Café Atlantico (p59)
> Georgia Brown's (p93)
> Palena (p112)
> Citronelle (p75)
> Sonoma Restaurant & Wine Bar (p50)

BEST OLD-SCHOOL DC JOINTS

> Hitching Post (p101)
> Florida Avenue Grill (p85)
> Jimmy T's (p50)
> Martin's Tavern (p78)
> Ben's Chili Bowl (p84)

BEST CHEAP CHOW

> W Domku (p101)
> Granville Moore's (p50)
> Busboys & Poets (p84)
> Comet Ping Pong (p112)
> Mixtec (p110)

Left We heart Hitching Post (p101) for soulful home cookin' like your mama used to make

KIDS

Oh, have you ever come to the right town.

Do cities such as Los Angeles and states like Florida offer as much fun for tiny dancers? Probably. But Washington tops those two in so many ways. First of all, Anaheim and Orlando aren't going to be nearly as healthy for the kids – like residents of any good East Coast city, Washingtonians are fans of this little thing called walking, and have the pedestrian pathways to prove it. The, um, National Mall (p34) immediately and obviously springs to mind, but let's not leave out Washington's glut of excellent parks, where wee ones can run, scream and cause chaos (or be their serene little selves) to their hearts' content. If you need to give little legs room to run, Rock Creek Park (p112) is a wilderness paradise, and as fresh air goes, make sure the tykes don't miss a ride in a donkey-pulled flatboat along the C&O Canal (p72).

Then there's the little fact that the fun Washington prepares for your pups can generally be appreciated for free. This, of course, applies to the entirety of the Smithsonian (p39), whose many museums almost all possess some sort of interpretive center for children. With that said, while you certainly don't have to pay to play in Washington, some of its best child-friendly museums charge admission – specifically the Newseum (p39) and the International Spy Museum (p56).

The sheer curatorial talent attracted by a city that has one of the best concentrations of museums in the world means exhibits are constantly being updated to increase their accessibility to kids. This even applies to sites outside the museum circuit, most notably the Library of Congress (p46), Capitol Visitor Center (p43) and that perennial favorite, the National Zoo (p112).

And while other towns might compete with DC in the fun stakes, what Washington slips in unnoticed, like the best PBS shows, is *education*. Why is this Lonely Planet author a Lonely Planet author? Because some of his earliest memories include rows of spidery Indonesian shadow puppets posing behind the glass in the Smithsonian's National Museum of Natural History (p39; pictured right), watching African dancers at the Kennedy Center (p95) and the international carnival that is the Smithsonian's Folklife festival (p23). In a similar vein, goodness knows how many careers in politics were launched by some first encounter with the Capitol (p43), or the right meeting in the right place near the White House lawn. Remember that grainy clip of young Bill Clinton shaking John F Kennedy's hand? Maybe your child can also grow up to become a figure of center-left reform.

And finally: don't underestimate how much kids can enjoy and even appreciate Washington's monuments and memorials. There's something about the latter's presence and grandiosity that is immediately accessible to children, whose comparative small stature enhances the feelings of awe and reverence these monuments inspire. At the same time, kids' imaginations are well positioned to accept the enormity of what they're viewing. Put plainly, it's always smile-inducing to go to the National Archives (p38) and hear some little girl whisper 'wow' the first time she sees the Declaration of Independence. This rule even applies to places you might initially consider child unfriendly, such as war memorials. Sometimes, a child's eye catches something unexpected, and very enlightening, in these powerful places – for example, this author's own realization, as a child, of how special quiet and contemplation could be during visits to the Vietnam Veterans Memorial (p40) with his Marine Corps veteran father.

BEST MUSEUMS FOR KIDS

> Smithsonian's National Museum of Natural History (p39; pictured above)
> National Air & Space Museum (p37)
> National Museum of American History (p38)
> International Spy Museum (p56)
> Newseum (p39)
> National Museum of the American Indian (p39)
> National Museum of African Art (p38)

TOP CHILD-FRIENDLY EXPERIENCES

> Visit the Lincoln Memorial, then chase ducks around the reflecting pool (p37)
> C&O Canal boat ride (p72), with a cupcake stop at Baked & Wired (p75)
> Ride to the top of the Washington Monument (p41)
> A slice and a game of table tennis at Comet Ping Pong (p112)
> Pandas at the National Zoo (p112)

CYCLING

By dint of its layout, terrible traffic, large green spaces and high population of educated environmentally friendly types, DC should be a city of cyclists. But it's not. There's some godawful gene imprinted in locals' DNA that says: it's cool to drive an hour to get the 3 miles from New York Ave to Dupont Circle. No, really.

To be fair, DC's excellent Metro system has helped keep locals on two feet as opposed to two wheels. But cycling should still be embraced by more District residents. On the bright side, the city of Washington, DC itself is all about biking; bus drivers and Metro gate operators don't give any guff for taking your bicycle on public transportation, and bike lanes are cropping up in an increasing web outside of the city center.

It's easy to see why Washington officials love bikes, and why more residents should get with the cycling program. DC really is excellent for pedal power. Offices are clustered in easily bike-accessible areas such as Foggy Bottom (p88) and Capitol Hill (p42), and the latter speaks to another plus to DC biking: incomparable scenery. Seriously – what did you bike past today? A traffic light? Because I cycled past the *freaking Washington Monument* (p41). Which brings up another advantage to two-wheeling around Washington: our enormous swathes of bike-friendly green lungs.

The National Mall (p34) is an obvious example: flat, stuffed with iconic symbols and connected to many of DC's most important workplaces.

From here you can easily access Ohio Dr, which starts at the Tidal Basin, the body of water overlooked by the Jefferson Memorial (p40), and runs in a 5-mile loop framed by the Washington Channel, Potomac River and a large sidewalk that's perfect for any cyclist, but particularly kids. If you find yourself on the west and northwest side of town, consider using Rock Creek Park (p112) as a circulatory commuting base; this enormous network of trails and woodland can be used as a wilderness biking backdrop for anyone commuting into, out of or between Adams Morgan (p104), Woodley Park and Upper Northwest.

While most time-conscious commuters would admit Washington is best accessed by the Metro, there are a few neighborhoods in town where a bicycle is more necessity than environmentally friendly alternative: Georgetown (p70), we're looking in your direction. With its lack of rail access, swathes of tree-lined wide residential boulevards and fine architectural eye candy, Georgetown is practically perfect for a day of cycling (although admittedly, the neighborhood does sprawl across large hills – you've been warned). But what truly makes Georgetown such a great cycling spot is the C&O Canal towpath (p72). Running, as it does, from here to Cumberland, the towpath is by nature of its former function (ie a canal) flat and wide, plus forested and scenic. It also runs in parts parallel to the **Capital Crescent Trail** (www.cctrail.com), which darts around Wisconsin Ave, through Rock Creek Park and up to the handsome suburb of Bethesda, MD. To access the Georgetown trailhead of the CC Trail, go to Water St (which becomes K St as you go further east) at the bottom of the Francis Scott Key Bridge; the trailhead is clearly marked.

Just across the Key Bridge, the Mt Vernon Trail runs 18 miles through northern Virginia to its namesake, the old digs of George Washington himself. This popular trail hugs the riverfront parallel to the District's attractive urban curves (all the more gussied up as they stretch over the Potomac) and through Old Town Alexandria (p52).

For those needing a guide, we recommend **Bike the Sites** (☎ 202-842-2453; www.bikethesites.com; 1100 Pennsylvania Ave, Old Post Office Pavilion; adult/child $40/30; Ⓜ Federal Triangle), which runs the best cycling tours of the capital. You may also want to check in with the **Washington Area Bicyclists' Association** (www.waba.org) before you visit for information on recommended trails, expansions, bike advocacy and more.

Left Riding the waterfront in Georgetown (p70), a neighborhood made for cycling

LITERARY DC

Washington doesn't lack for literary biographers. This is a town that attracts a surfeit of intellectual energy, much of it geared toward professions that rely heavily on wordplay. Journalists, lawyers, politicians et al have found expression beyond their careers by turning sharp authors' eyes onto the corridors of power and rain-slicked alleys of the capital. The above are joined by a cadre of homegrown writing talent drawn from DC, Virginia and Maryland, all of which seem to produce storytellers in good proportion to their population.

With that said, it's the rare DC writer who can untangle this city's many knots – Anacostia crime, congressional scandal, expanding bourgeoisification etc – into one narrative thread. That's not necessarily a bad thing. Washington's diversity is her strength, but that same quality lends her the divisions that drive a good story's tension. After all, it's not the fault of writers that the Capitol and some of the neighborhoods in her shadow are so removed from each other they don't seem cut out for the same story.

Perhaps that's why, while there are plenty of novels set in DC, few claim to be DC novels, per se. On the other hand, the capital generates a huge amount of short stories. Some of our favorites have been written by former *Washington Post* reporter Ward Just (FYI, a lot of DC's best writers have cut their teeth at the *Post*). His collection *The Congressman Who Loved Flaubert* is as dry, tragicomic, intelligent and human a rendering as you'll find of the Hill, as is his novel *Echo House*.

For the same scene and setting cast under the considerably brighter glare of chick lit, we'd recommend *Sammy's Hill* and the sequel *Sammy's House* by Kristin Gore, daughter of…oh, who was that guy again…and in any case, a decent dish on life in political Washington for those needing a read with a brightly colored cover.

Good writers search out conflict to give their stories significance and drive, but for many, the battles on the Hill are too bloodless. So they cross the Anacostia or venture up Rhode Island Ave into Northeast. This task of digging into DC's underclass has often been upheld by authors of the crime and noir genre, and *DC Noir,* a collection of short stories edited by George Pelecanos, is as good an introduction to this world (literary and actual) as you'll find. As a bonus, the collection funnels some of the city's finest contemporary writing talent, including Kenji Jasper and Jennifer Howard, into one book. Pelecanos himself is one of the city's best scribes, an author who peppers his work with geographic references visitors can learn from and insiders can appreciate. *Right to Rain* and *The Night Gardener* are both excellent examples of his work, lessons on and adventures in DC's hard edge, and ripping good reads to boot.

Much of DC's best literary canon is nonfiction, direct commentary on America itself and, often, penned by her First Citizens. Here we're specifically referring to the letters and speeches of presidents such as Thomas Jefferson and Abraham Lincoln, whose work possesses both insight and depth of prose we're hoping a certain Mr Obama can match (*Dreams of My Father,* which critics from *Time* to the *Guardian* have called the best memoir by a major American politician in decades, seems a good start). In the meantime, while we've seen great reads that illuminate both DC's politics and predators, we're still awaiting the writer who can capture what Washington is becoming: a city still marked by divisions between haves and have-nots but not defined by them (if ever it was).

HISTORICAL HIGHLIGHTS

> *The Federalist Papers,* by Alexander Hamilton, James Madison and John Jay
> *Life and Times of Frederick Douglass,* by Frederick Douglass
> *Democracy,* by Henry Adams
> *The Gilded Age,* by Mark Twain
> *Washington DC,* by Gore Vidal

HARLEM RENAISSANCE TO INNER CITY: BOOKS ON BLACK DC

> *Cane,* by Jean Toomer
> *The New Negro,* by Alain Locke
> *Lost in the City,* by Edward P Jones
> *Long Distance Life,* by Marita Golden
> *The Turnaround,* by George Pelecanos

JUST PRETTY POLITICAL

> *All the President's Men,* by Bob Woodward and Carl Bernstein
> *Shelley's Heart,* by Charles McCarry
> *Echo House,* by Ward Just
> *Advise and Consent,* by Allen Drury
> *Blinded by the Right,* by David Brock

EVERYONE NEEDS AN EASY READ

> *The Washingtonienne,* by Jessica Cutler
> *Fear and Loathing on the Campaign Trail '72,* by Hunter S Thompson
> *Sammy's Hill,* by Kristin Gore
> *Below the Beltway* columns, by Gene Weingarten in the *Washington Post Magazine*
> *The Audacity of Hope,* by Barack Obama

BARS

When Andrew Jackson swore the oath of office back in 1800, the self-proclaimed populist dispensed with pomp and circumstance and, quite literally, threw a raging kegger. Folks got so gone they started looting art from the White House.

The historical lesson to be learned is DC loves a drink, and these days it enjoys said tipples in many incarnations besides executive-mansion-trashing throwdowns. If you've never been here, you may imagine glasses of wine in a slick-ish resto-bar, and yes, such drinks are drunk while decisions of the day are determined. Many restaurants, from the chic gastro-experimental to the down-and-out diner, also double as some of DC's best bars by night. But as politico bantering and policy hashing goes, you have a better chance of catching your congressperson (or much more likely, their aides) in a dark-paneled, cozy joint in the vicinity of Capitol Hill (p51). We're not sure why; it may be a side effect of DC's anti-elitism elitism, wherein everyone tries to come off as one of the guys – and about that appropriations bill Bob?

Today, DC is increasingly (and excitingly) integrating the federal capital with the city that has always been here, and like anywhere, said city doesn't survive on business bars alone. Make no mistake: local pubs are as common as lobbyist lounges. With that said, politics is interwoven into the capital psyche, so if you want, you can still have a Pabst in a corner hole and get into an in-depth discussion on the survival chances of that Darfur aid package in the upcoming committee meeting – or scrap the business (and by business, we mean politics) talk altogether. Spots such as Mr Smith's (p79) and Dan's Café (p111) offer this uniquely Washingtonian amalgamation of work and political pleasure.

Since the 1990s, the traditional locus of DC's barflies has been a well-worn path running from U St (p86) up 18th St into the heart of Adams Morgan (p111), with the occasional detour allowed for some more cerebral talk and tipple in Dupont Circle (p67). You'll find it all here, from hip lounges to jazz bars that hosted John Coltrane and Ella Fitzgerald (p87). But as the city becomes more middle class, its drinking scene – or that part of it that isn't just neighborhood hangouts – has expanded. Stretching from Columbia Heights into Northeast (p102) and east of Capitol Hill onto H St (p51), many hip but grit spots have opened their doors. These are some of the best bars around, not just for their shots (although those are good), but for the effort they make at mixing DC's longtimers with the creative class types increasingly streaming into town.

You can judge whether or not the effort is working, or if all of the above is cover talk, and all these new bars add up to is more gentrification. We're not so cynical. The multiracial but all-DC crowd laughing, slamming shots, hitting on and hooking up in bars and resto-bars such as the Looking Glass (p102) and the Argonaut (p49) tells us this town's tensions can potentially be washed away with a Yuengling beer. And to be frank, as pretentious as political talk can be, it's kind of refreshing knowing the guy next to you can expound on not just the 'Skins latest loss to the Cowboys, but also Fenty's plans for Ward 8 *and* what he thinks of the First Lady's new dress.

BEST BARS TO FEEL LIKE A LOCAL IN

> Looking Glass Lounge (p102)
> Raven (p102)
> Red Derby (p103)
> Dan's Café (p111)
> Marvin (p86)

BEST RESTAURANTS DOUBLING AS WATERING HOLES

> Cork (p85)
> W Domku (p101)
> Kramerbooks & Afterwords Café (p67)
> Granville Moore's (p50)
> Brickskeller (p67)

Left Kramerbooks & Afterwords Café (p67): a mixed business (books, bistro and booze) perfect for a mixed drink

NIGHTLIFE

We've studiously avoided a certain type of Washington institution thus far, but the 'Nightlife' snapshot heralds its unavoidable arrival: the silly DC nightclub. It's usually located somewhere near Downtown – K St or Penn Quarter – and features long lines (even if no one's inside; must keep up appearances), jerk bouncers, watered-down drinks, guys who yell 'dude!' and girls who…well, yell.

Let us stress, emphatically, that there is more to DC's after hours than the above, but too many fresh arrivals get caught up in it. We like to get dressed up as much as the next party person, but we also like a little weirdness with our night on the town. When our hips preach like Shakira, we groove in spots such as Chief Ike's (p113), where Day-of-the-Dead-on-drugs murals stare from the walls. If that's not strange enough for you, how about the permanent freak show at Palace of Wonders (p53)?

If you just need to feel as good as you look and dance near, flirt with and possibly pick up people of a like mind-set, DC's got you covered. Try the 18th Street Lounge (p68), any of the nightspots open along the other stretch of 18th St – the one that runs through Adams Morgan (p104) – or U St (p86), including the crowded, hormonal deck of Local 16 (p87). There are also plenty of clubs of the mega-venue variety in DC's outer reaches (you know, the ones where life is an Usher video, starring you), including **Love** (☎ 202-636-9030; 1350 Okie St) and **Fur** (☎ 202-842-3401; 33 Patterson St NE). You'll need a taxi or your own wheels to reach these places. Keep in mind that many of the bars we've reviewed double as clubs/lounges on weekends.

If you need a cerebral start to your evening, DC offers plenty of ways to stimulate mind and senses, many free. Check www.citypaper.com for gigs such as experimental music at the Hirshhorn (p36), world dance at the Kennedy Center (p95) and punk DJs playing the Black Cat backstage (p87).

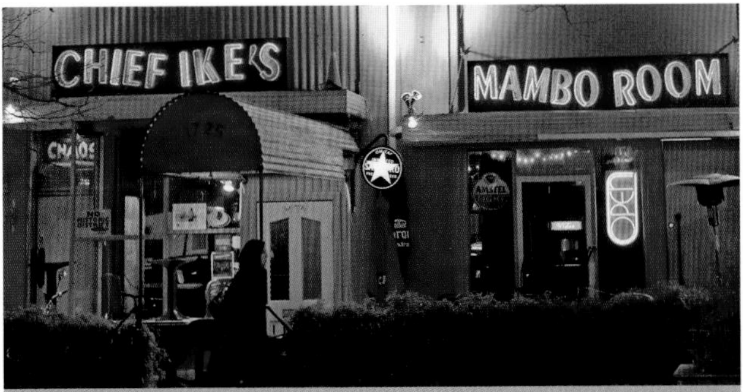

BEST BARS-TURNED-CLUBS COME WEEKENDS

> Marvin (p86)
> Big Hunt (p67)
> Madam's Organ (p111)
> Reef (p111)
> Wonderland (p103)

WHERE TO LOOK FINE 'N SHAKE THAT FINE THANG

> 18th Street Lounge (p68)
> Mie N Yu (p78)
> Local 16 (see above)
> Ghana Café (p113)
> Café St-Ex (p86)

Top Left Friday-night crush outside Saki on Adams Morgan's (p104) 18th St **Above** Cha-cha at Chief Ike's (p113)

LIVE MUSIC

Sorry to harp on the theme again, but herein is another example of Washington, city of many cities.

When it comes to live music, Washington's personality splits in several directions. The city doesn't just split along racial lines, but age ones as well. There's the evening-wear elegance of watching flamenco at the Kennedy Center (p95); the dance-floor thrum of *makossa* (Cameroonian music) blended with hip-hop in a corner club in Adams Morgan (p113); punk stripping the paint in the Red & Black (p51); and jazz notes stretching like silk over your whiskey in Bohemian Caverns (p87).

And yet…what city doesn't have a variety of musical tastes? You know what? We take it back: Washington's musical diversity is strong, but in this case, that diversity doesn't lead to (too many) divisions. We've seen white former diplomats nodding along to P-Square in West African clubs, black doormen with Mohawks bouncing at jazz-type bars frequented by white college students, and African American children entranced by the Marine Corps band on the steps of the Capitol.

So is there a DC sound? No more and no less than there is an American one. We don't swing to any one rhythm but all of them, and if the setting is cerebral, we're as happy with nationally renowned opera as Ellington beats born around the block. And that diversity extends to venue as much as artist, because we'll listen anywhere – from corner dives to grand ballrooms to the front yard of America herself.

WHERE TO CATCH CAPITAL SHOWS

- Hirshhorn Museum & Sculpture Garden (p36)
- 9:30 Club (p87)
- Bohemian Caverns (p87)
- Kennedy Center (p95)
- Black Cat (p87)

LEGENDARY DC PERFORMERS & VENUES

- Marian Anderson, steps of the Lincoln Memorial, 1939
- Ruth Brown at Bohemian Caverns, 1930s
- Thievery Corporation at the 18th Street Lounge, 1990s
- Fugazi in the 9:30 Club, 1980s
- Itzhak Perlman, Yo-Yo Ma, Anthony McGill and Gabriela Montero, Barack Obama inauguration, the Capitol, 2009

SHOPPING

Shopping styles are inextricably tied up with neighborhood geography in this town. For those seeking high-end, brand-name affirmation, look no further than Georgetown (p73), which also contains DC's original strip of interior design boutiques in Cady's Alley (p74). In some ways, Dupont Circle (p65) offers much of a muchness, although the tags are not as brand conscious and the designer homewares not quite as mind-bogglingly expensive. Still, at the end of the day, Dupont is yuppie paradise.

In contrast, you'll find nary a brand name along U St (p83) and in Adams Morgan (p106); this is where the indie boutiques get chic and the accessories for your home are plucked from cool attics rather than sleek Scandinavian magazines. As these areas continually gentrify (and rents climb), expect their shopping scenes to become glitzier/blander in coming years.

Speaking of which…if you're in need of malls/Gap/Starbucks/blah, be aware that Penn Quarter (p57), especially in the area around the Verizon Center/Chinatown, is approaching Anywhere America. More interesting in this vicinity are the gift shops in DC's museums, which really are – no, really! – some of the coolest museum stores you'll find, practically perfect places for selecting your favorite capital-worthy souvenir.

BEST DC SOUVENIRS

- > Rhinestone Obama cap, Skynear & Co (p109)
- > Nats scarf (because someday…), Nationals Stadium (p46)
- > Vintage campaign mementos ('Quayle '92!'), Political Americana (p58)
- > Ward Just or George Pelecanos novels, Politics & Prose (p112)
- > A tobacco pipe – just a tobacco pipe, officer! – shaped like your state, B&K Newsstand (p106)

MAGNIFICENT MUSEUM STORE GIFTS

- > Fake dinosaur bones, Smithsonian's National Museum of Natural History (p39)
- > Designer bowls, Corcoran Gallery of Art (p90)
- > Plush News Hound toys, Newseum (p39)
- > Prints, Smithsonian American Art Museum (p56)
- > Astronaut ice cream, National Air & Space Museum (p37)

FASHION

Thanks, Michelle.

Obama, that is. Remember that kinda sexy yet refined one-shoulder number she wore to all the inauguration balls after Barack got sworn in? Or her general projection of business-suited power mixed with approachability and yes, feminine allure?

Michelle O and Jackie O: reminding the rest that yes, Washingtonians can dress.

Look, not to sound bitter or anything, but it's not like Washington is known for its style, and there's a bit of precedent behind this popular ruling. Locals remember that one summer when it seemed like *every guy in the city* wore the same blue-striped-shirt-and-khaki combination out every night of the week (and to be fair, lots of guys haven't changed that look). Yeah, Washington has still got its striped shirt, and don't get us started on the twin-set and pearls look of a certain type of Capitol Hill woman, or those staffers with collars so starched they could open a bakery. Of course, the above completely discounts black DC style, which ranges from sho-lows (ankle-length shorts) to Sunday church crowns (hats) that would put Royal Ascot to shame.

Still, as Washington gets flooded with new arrivals attracted by jobs, Obama ideology, whatever, Washingtonians are getting more experimental with their outfits. True, expression here has traditionally been measured more by your particular cause than clothes, but locals have realized they can be the dedicated activists they are and still look good in the process, and even – well, if you're a First Lady – set some examples for those snoots and suits up in NYC.

BEST BOUTIQUES

> Nana (p84)
> Redeem (p84)
> Relish (p74)
> Circle Boutique (p83)
> Green & Blue (p65)

WHERE DC'S BEST/MOST INTERESTINGLY DRESSED IMPRESS

> Attending White House balls
> Over drinks at Mie N Yu (p78)
> Heading to work on Capitol Hill
> While getting flirty at the 18th Street Lounge (p68)
> After showing off new tattoos at Palace of Wonders (p53)

GAY DC

Sitting as it does at the ideological and geographic crossroads of American activism, liberalism and conservatism, Washington has a mixed civil rights record. But at least in regards to GLBT (Gay-Lesbian-Bisexual-Transgender) issues, the capital has an admirable (if not perfect) track record of progressivism and a fair bit of scene to boot, the latter still very much centered in Dupont Circle (p62).

Thanks to Washington's obvious political persuasion, the local gay community isn't as obsessed with pushing the behavior envelope as San Francisco or Key West are. In DC, the rainbow stereotype consists of well-groomed professionals and activists concerned with passing HIV-education bills. That's not to say folks don't have fun, though – the party rages from Cobalt (p69) to Phase 1 (p51), and during Capital Pride (p23) you'll see the usual carnival of leather and drag (although that guy in the biker leathers may have a Libertarian party button pinned to his, er, codpiece).

Washington's black community has traditionally been of two minds on homosexuality: socially conservative thanks to strong church ties, yet understanding of oppression. From the early 20th century, when Georgia Douglas Johnson's Saturday-night salons on S St NW hosted luminaries including Angelina Weld Grimké, Alain Locke and Langston Hughes, to today's DC Black Pride festival (p23), the capital backdrop has long been used to highlight the fight for, and celebrate the acceptance of, racial and sexuality-based civil rights in America.

Proudly parading the rainbow flag toward Washington Monument during Capital Pride (p23)

GREEN SPACE

Most city centers are defined by a block of businesses – even New York's Central Park isn't so much of an anchor as a diversion from Manhattan's urban wilderness – but Washington's heart (and in a way, America's) is green. An occasionally sandy, scraggly green, yes, but grass and water and trees nonetheless. The National Mall (p34; for that is what we are referring to) is DC's cornerstone by any measure, and to Washingtonians, it's as much a symbol of DC's love of nature as it is of the Democratic Adventure.

The capital has always been structured to reflect both the ideals of the nation and the urban execution of the perfect republic, and planners from Pierre L'Enfant (the original city planner of DC) to current mayor Adrian Fenty have considered the inclusion of nature integral to this experiment. We're not just talking about preserving the outdoors in the midst of the city, although DC does so, most notably in enormous Rock Creek Park (p112). There's also the desire to collect and preserve America's flora in her capital, and broker coexistence, even a synergy, between two seemingly opposing energies: urban and natural.

To whit: Malcolm X Park (p106) spilling over the Fall Line and almost onto 16th St, the National Arboretum's (p98) gardens clumping like green hands pawing through Northeast's residential blocks, and any of the countless tree-lined avenues of Northwest, which all manage to make the capital occasionally come off as a devoted grandma pottering around her garden.

FAVORITE WASHINGTON WALKS

> From the Freer and Sackler Galleries (p36) to the Thomas Jefferson Memorial (p40)
> Around the Sylvan Theater in the National Arboretum (p98)
> Along the C&O Canal (p72)
> Through the gardens of Dumbarton Oaks (p72)
> Under shedding cherry blossoms in spring (p22)

OTHER OUTDOOR ACTIVITIES

> Cutting through Malcolm X Park to get from U St to Adams Morgan (p106)
> Naps under trees near the Smithsonian Castle (p39)
> Getting your knees dirty in Rock Creek Park (p112)
> A stroll through the Franklin Delano Roosevelt Memorial (p36)
> Frisbee on the National Mall (p34)

SPORTS

Republicans. Democrats. Diplomats. Environmentalists. Industrialists. Immigrants. White. Black. Brown. Locals all.

Love sports.

These are the ties that bind, folks: not monuments or elections or inaugurations or even Chuck Brown on a summer day. Nope: it's burgundy and gold, the colors of DC's beloved Redskins; the Capitals on ice, who won the National Hockey League's Southeast Division title in 2008 for the first time in eight years; the pretty much perennially failure-prone Wizards (how can a city that loves street ball so much suck so bad in the NBA?); DC United, still by far one of Major League Soccer's most popular and successful clubs; the Howard Bisons and Georgetown Hoyas and other university teams, along with their rabid student body fans; and the Nationals, who have finally freed Washingtonians from the drive to Baltimore for baseball.

If you're around for a bit, try and catch a game. The nation's capital comes together in ways unexpected and touching when sports are at stake; it's about the only event that gets as pumped as politics, and it's probably more accessible, if not quite as cutthroat.

WHERE TO WATCH

> The Redskins (NFL) – FedExField, Landover Maryland
> The Nationals (MLB) – Nationals Stadium (p46)
> The Wizards (NBA), Capitals (NHL) and Georgetown Basketball – Verizon Center (p61)
> DC United (MLB) – RFK Stadium (p53)

GREAT DC SPORTS MOMENTS

> Patrick Ewing's Hoyas win the NCAA championship, 1984
> Redskins take Superbowl XXII 42-10, 1988
> George W Bush throws first pitch to the new Washington Nationals and a new MLB team is born, 2005
> DC United wins the Concacaf Cup (International Club Soccer championship for North and Central America and the Caribbean), 1998
> 'Skins win their first Superbowl (XVII) led by the Hogs, 1983

ART

We were about to launch into an essay on DC's gallery goings-on when it struck: there's another art world in Washington, so obvious that to long-time residents it's not even considered a 'scene.' We're referring, of course, to the fine and modern arts concentrated in Washington's museums. True, those institutions may not offer the exclusive local talent that constitutes the traditional definition of 'scene,' but Washington's official aesthetic style should, to a degree, reflect America's. Some citizens criticize pieces displayed at the Smithsonian as conservative, but there is much to say in their defense: some exhibits, particularly in the National Portrait Gallery (p56), are pretty cutting-edge, and the Smithsonian is trying to encourage love of the arts among Americans as a populace, not satisfy avant-garde envelope-pushing. And you simply can't ignore the masterpieces preening in their gorgeous spaces such as the Hirshhorn (p36), east wing of the National Gallery (p38), Corcoran (p90) and the Phillips Collection (p64).

Then there are the aforementioned local studios, a result of this town attracting educated types who either appreciate good art or need outlets for their creativity. The freshest galleries crop up in U St (p80) and the newly gentrifying frontier of Columbia Heights and Northeast DC (p96). One of the best places to begin delving into Washington's local aesthetic is the great local artist/designer cooperative of Dekka (p83), and no exposure to Washington-area artists is complete without a visit to Alexandria's Torpedo Factory Art Center (p52).

THE BEST OF THE OFFICIAL ART SCENE

> National Portrait Gallery (p56)
> Renwick Gallery (p91)
> Corcoran Gallery of Art (p90)
> Phillips Collection (p64)
> Annexes of the Smithsonian American Art Museum (p56)

GREAT GRAFFITI, DC MURALS & ART OF THAT ILK

> Barack Obama's hopeful face on the wall of Marvin (p86)
> Duke Ellington portrait, 1200 U St, near Ben's Chili Bowl (p84)
> Frederick Douglass mural, 1204 Massachusetts Ave
> Westminster Playground community art, 907 Westminster St NW
> T-shirts air-brushed with local graffiti tags, U Street Flea Market (p84)

THEATER

In Washington, presidents have been killed in the theater – specifically Abraham Lincoln in the famous **Ford's** (www.fordstheatre.org) – and been masters of it. Washington is full of the drama and acting and artifice that comprise the most fundamental definition of theater: the art of convincing people that you feel a certain way about something. District citizens are the subject of daily political theater, ranging from federal sleight of hand to promises from police to step up patrols in local wards.

Locals are trained to see through an act; ergo they appreciate a high level of performance art. It helps that Washington has such a diverse range of stage lovers: educated types who patronize the likes of the **Shakespeare Theatre** (www.shakespearetheatre.org) and the Folger (p46), high-end production-philes at the National Theatre (p60) and niche performance-goers at the Pulitzer Prize–winning **Studio** (www.studiotheatre.org). Immigrants give the diaspora experience dramatic voice in spaces such as **Gala** (www.galatheatre.org), while an appreciation of global perspectives is fed by regular international performances held in the Kennedy Center (p95). The cutting edge of experimentation plays out under lights at the **Woolly Mammoth** (www.woollymammoth.net), a palpable sense of African American history exudes from the **Lincoln** (www.thelincolntheatre.org) and a show under the stars at the **Carter Barron** (www.nps.gov/rocr/cbarron) is always a family-friendly treat.

Yup – Washingtonians can see through an act. But that doesn't mean they don't enjoy a good one when they see it.

Bard-o-philes rejoice: Folger Shakespeare Library & Theatre (p46)

POLITICS

The District was built for and lives on politics, and all Washingtonians can talk the issues. But sometimes we get sick of politics, which may be why over a million people, the majority from DC, Maryland and Virginia, crowding onto the National Mall for Barack Obama's inauguration in February 2009 was so inspiring. For so many of DC's own, it marked a renewal of faith, and if anyone deserves to disbelieve, it's the people who haven't just seen the underbelly of the system, but those who drive by it every day.

Washington is a town where the buzz isn't just about sports or shopping or stocks, but a nuanced analysis of what makes America, well, America. Some locals understand there may be tensions between the new Eritrean and Ethiopian neighbors because they may have worked in East Africa. Young staffers become wise when, from senatorial proximity, they realize a compromise can be both a way of selling out, but also the only way forward on an issue. It's thrilling when the girl or guy you're talking to in a bar, isn't just a pretty face, but someone who manages debt-relief programs for a country you backpacked in. That's all politics. And that's all DC.

WHERE TO SEE POLITICS IN ACTION

> During congressional committee hearings (p43)
> Sunday brunch at Georgia Brown's (p93)
> Evening dinner at the Prime Rib (p94)
> Happy hour at the Hawk & Dove (p51)
> With protestors in front of the White House (p91)

POLITICALSPEAK 101

> Filibuster – the art of delaying the passage of a bill by talking it to death, now slang for any delaying action
> Gerrymander – when officials redraw electoral boundaries for their own benefit
> Pork barrel – hitching funding, often for roads, dams and bridges, to surefire bills that have nothing to do with said projects
> Red/Blue/Purple America – the clotted colors of the US' political map: respectively, conservative, liberal and somewhere-in-between America
> Flack – professional PR types who 'spin' the events of the day in favor of their clients

>BACKGROUND

Main Reading Room at the stunning neoclassical Library of Congress (p46)

BACKGROUND

HISTORY

FOUNDING THE FEDERAL CITY

The Patawomeck and Piscataway nations of the Tidewater region hunted deer, farmed corn and gathered oysters and fish from the Chesapeake watershed near the Potomac River prior to European arrival. Despite the disease and displacement that followed, both of the above tribes live on, in Virginia and Maryland respectively, today.

White settlers began farming plots of land in the area that would become the capital as early as the end of the 17th century. The geographic location marks the fall line between the Piedmont Plateau and the Atlantic Coastal Plain, and as such, was as far as boats going upriver could travel in the 18th century. As a result, the area that would become Georgetown served as a port for Maryland tobacco destined for the colonial interior.

Following the American Revolution, the new nation had a difficult time deciding from where to administer itself. Philadelphia was the original choice, but when Pennsylvania governor John Dickinson refused to defend Congress from protestors in 1783, new options were cast about. Regional rivalries were multiple and deep, and to address them a central location between the Northern and Southern colonies was proposed, a federally administered district 'not exceeding 10 miles square (100 square miles).' All eyes drifted to the Maryland–Virginia border. George Washington himself sank some beers with local landowners in Suter's tavern in Georgetown and persuaded them to sell their holdings to Congress for $66 an acre.

The land around Georgetown and Alexandria was ceded to the federal government and, in 1791, surveyed by a team led by Major Andrew Ellicott that included African American Benjamin Banneker. The borders of the eventually surveyed square would enclose the District of Columbia; inside would be the City of Washington. (Since then the city has grown to the point it has all but spilled outside of the District's borders; a Brookings Institution report recommends Washington, DC needs triple its originally offered space to have a viable tax base.)

The initial design of the city was awarded to Pierre L'Enfant, who envisaged a town of canals and state-named diagonal avenues connecting roundabouts and traffic circles. But L'Enfant clashed with city commissioners and left the project, to be replaced by Ellicott of the survey team.

The latter laid his idea for the capital directly over L'Enfant's, and thus, on top of diagonal avenues such as Pennsylvania and Rhode Island, Washington is a grid of north–south numbered and east–west lettered streets.

A free black man may have helped survey Washington, but thousands of enslaved ones were tasked with building it. By 1800 the new capital was muddy, half-constructed and miserable, and for the first time, the home of an American president: John Adams.

BURNING & REBUILDING

Officially, Americans learn the War of 1812 was fought because the British Navy was bullying American merchant ships and shanghaiing American sailors. Another version is that the USA got into a fight because it decided to try and invade British Canada while a simultaneous confederation of British-backed Native American tribes formed in the west, intent on halting breakneck American expansionism.

The USA was turned back from Canada; the Native American alliance was broken; the British saw an opportunity and tried to take back their old colony, burning Washington and its new Capitol in 1814. But a little Frenchman named Napoleon was a more pressing concern to the UK, so Washington's ashes were left smoldering. There was no guarantee those ashes would ever be cleaned up; a demoralized motion to abandon the city and select a new capital only failed in Congress by nine votes. Britain redeemed itself, in a sense, when in 1826 English scientist James Smithson – who never visited America – left a half-million dollar endowment to the USA that would become the basis of the Smithsonian Institution.

The city was eventually rebuilt, largely by black hands, and slaves and free blacks (including some slave-owning free blacks) clustered around the capital. For a long period, Washington was the premier slave-trading city in North America. Race relations were always a tense and muddled thing, and overlaying them were the geographic tensions between an industrializing North that, for reasons humanitarian and economic, was increasingly rejecting slavery, and a South grown more dependent on it. The slave trade was outlawed in Washington in1850, but not before Virginia reabsorbed (or 'retroceded') the slave port of Alexandria (slavery itself as a practice was outlawed in 1862).

Issues of secession and slavery came to a head in 1861 when the country was riven by Civil War. The capital of the Union lay directly across the Potomac from the home of Robert E Lee, general of the Confederate Army. Spies filtered in and out of the city, and while it was only raided by the enemy once (in 1864), hundreds of thousands of Americans died in a radius drivable in barely an hour in any direction of the city: Manassas, Fredericksburg, Chancellorsville and Antietam. When Abraham Lincoln was re-elected in 1864, he swore the oath of office under a newly constructed Capitol dome. A little over a year later, the Civil War was won, and a few days after that, Lincoln was murdered in Ford's Theater by disgruntled actor John Wilkes Booth.

INTO THE 20TH CENTURY

In 1871 the then technically separate cities of Georgetown and Washington plus the 'county' of Washington were combined by Congress into Washington, DC, administered by a Board of Public Works (BPW). Via railways (the B&O), canals (the C&O) and public works promoted by BPW-head Alexander Shepherd, the city built itself into just that: a place of paved roads, public services and the like, rather than a muddy confluence of streets and shacks. Shepherd, starting a grand tradition, outspent the city budget, causing Congress to wrestle control of Washington back, but his efforts helped forge an urban identity for the District that had previously been lacking.

The federal capital you see today was created, in both form and function, throughout much of the 20th century. Inspired by the 'City Beautiful' movement, which equated public aesthetics with civic virtue, the 1901 McMillan Plan created the National Mall and its facade of neoclassical marble. The combination of Shepherd's necessary infrastructure construction and the McMillan Plan's beautification finally forged a marketable brand and skyline of Washington that, in many ways, persist to this day.

The Great Depression and the Franklin Roosevelt years were, in their way, good ones for the capital. The New Deal both employed thousands to improve city public works and brought more federal agency staff into the vicinity of the city, expanding its profile, economy and population with whole residential blocks of office workers and the support and service industries that followed them. The same phenomenon came on the heels of WWII, which finished with the construction of the Pentagon.

SEGREGATION, CIVIL RIGHTS & HOME RULE

The capital of the free world adhered to the racial segregation polices of the South throughout much of the 20th century, but it was also, by dint of its role, destined for activism, protests and marches. Public recreational areas such as parks were largely desegregated in 1954, followed by DC public schools, the first to be forcibly integrated by the Eisenhower administration. In 1957, as wealthier whites moved to outlying suburbs and northbound blacks moved into the neighborhoods, Washington became the first majority African American city in the country. Martin Luther King gave his 'I Have a Dream' speech on the steps of the Lincoln Memorial in 1963; five years later, following his assassination, much of DC burned against a backdrop of race riots centered on U St. It took decades for some neighborhoods to rebuild in the wake of the chaos.

In the meantime Washington was redefining the way she managed herself. The city took on a more politically liberal cast when the JFK administration attracted thousands of idealistic, service-minded Americans to DC. In 1961 Washington was granted electors in the electoral college, guaranteeing citizens some say in the outcome of the national elections. In 1973 Congress passed the Home Rule act, which grants Washington greater autonomy, and residents responded by electing African American Walter Washington to the office of mayor. Three years later, the DC Metro (subway) started carrying passengers, largely from the suburbs into downtown offices.

With white flight came depopulation and abandonment; with these factors came more poverty and crime. During the '80s and '90s DC became infamous for often sitting atop the nation's murder rate statistics. The 1990 arrest of mayor Marion Barry with a crack pipe in a DC hotel room didn't help the city's reputation as a law-abiding, well-run capital. But things eventually improved. Under mayor Anthony Williams deficits were turned into surpluses, gentrification began to change the face of the capital and crime fell. The middle class and young professionals began moving into new condos in Dupont and around U St.

When the District was told to use some of its funds from the Homeland Security budget to pay for George W Bush's second inauguration in 2005, a number of residents objected. They had already voted for John Kerry by a margin of 89% – the highest democratic percentage in the country, until residents voted for Barack Obama by a 92% margin. The election of Obama has replicated the Camelot atmosphere of the 1960s, and on January 30, 2009, Reuters publicly pondered if Washington would eclipse Wall St in importance (if it hasn't already) as Americans increasingly lose faith in business and seem willing to believe in their government in levels unheard of since the days of FDR and JFK.

LIFE AS A WASHINGTONIAN

This is as good a time as any to be a Washingtonian – depending on what type of Washingtonian you happen to be. If you're working a 'DC' job – that is, for the government or in one of the think tanks, law firms, media outlets, universities or international organizations that are all based here as a result of the government – then you're in an elite crowd. You earn one of the highest per capita incomes in the country, your colleagues constitute the greatest concentration of knowledge workers in America, with some 22% holding an advanced degree, and as of 2008, the city you live in has the lowest unemployment of America's 50 largest metropolitan areas.

You pay for the above privilege, of course. Rents in downtown DC are rarely below four figures a month (the average hovers around $1100), and basic commodities such as groceries and oil tend to be more expensive inside the District than in Maryland and Virginia. You go out a lot, for business and pleasure; this is a city built on both power lunches and power drinks after work, and the temptation to expense is high and often given in to. You probably vote Democrat but then again there's that chance you're working at the Heritage Foundation or for some Republican up on the Hill. Your address very likely ends in the letters 'NW,' which indicate Washington's posh Northwest quadrant, although you may also live on Capitol Hill, in which case you are technically in the Southeast.

Actually, we should point out that if you fit the above profile, there's a good chance you don't technically live in Washington, DC at all, particularly if you have a family. In this case, odds are you're settled into one of the suburbs of northern Virginia and Maryland, which means that you don't pay taxes to DC despite working inside the city, which further means you are resented by many Washingtonians. If you live inside the city, you probably take the Metro to work; if you live outside in the 'burbs, you probably should take the Metro to work, but very likely drive instead.

If you don't fit the above profile – if you're in DC's underclass – the picture isn't as rosy, although it's better than what it was. In this case, despite that low unemployment rate, there's an 18% chance you live below the poverty line (compared to a 12% national statistic). Despite all those knowledge workers, you're 10% more likely than the average American to operate on a low literacy level.

TOP DC FILMS

Most movies on Washington focus on the workings of the government as opposed to city life. The best, exemplified by some of the below, combine the two themes. For an overview of books on DC and some of the capital's best authors, see the Literary DC Snapshot, p128.

- *Mr Smith Goes to Washington* (1939) – the quintessential Washington, DC political drama of the little guy, portrayed by Jimmy Stewart at his most…American, standing up to all those big bad special interests.
- *All the President's Men* (1976) – the excellent drama that follows the Watergate investigation of Bob Woodward and Carl Bernstein, in which some little guys really did bring down some big bad special interests – the Nixon presidency.
- *The Exorcist* (1973) – eeek. Still one of our favorite scary movies. See what happens when a little girl in Georgetown gets possessed by the demon Pazuzu. Answer: evil, evil, guys falling down stairs, evil.
- *Spy Game* (2001) – while not exclusively set in DC, this is one of the better what's-it-like-to-work-for-the-CIA thrillers out there, and includes some excellent atmosphere shots of the capital.
- *Legally Blonde 2* (2003) – Reese Witherspoon gives us the chick-flick take on the last-honest-American-cleaning-up-the-capital genre.
- *Head of State* (2003) – Chris Rock plays a DC alderman (municipal councilman) who ends up running for, and winning the presidency of the United States. Smarter commentary than you might think.
- *Bulworth* (1998) – Warren Beatty plays a Democratic senator who takes a contract out on his own life and then finds himself liberated to finally speak the truth he's been holding back all his life.
- *Wedding Crashers* (2005) – Owen Wilson and Vince Vaughn strike a blow for testosterone in this buddy movie about DC divorce lawyers sleeping their way through capital-area wedding bashes.
- *Talk to Me* (2007) – see the other side of DC in this ripping biopic of local radio DJ and ex-con Ralph 'Petey' Green, who hosted one of the city's most popular morning shows during the racially charged 1960s and '70s.

There's about an overall 15% chance you're an immigrant, and if so, you could be from anywhere, although odds are on Central America, particularly El Salvador, or East Africa or south Asia. Technically, Washington is about 57% black, but of the aforementioned privileged classes, a much higher proportion are white or Asian. With that said, DC has one of the largest middle- and upper-class black communities in America, although many of these wealthier African Americans have moved out to the Prince George's County suburbs.

DIRECTORY

TRANSPORTATION

ARRIVAL & DEPARTURE

AIR

The **Super Shuttle** (☎ 800-258-3826; www.supershuttle.com) runs door-to-door van service from all three of the airports following; call ahead or check the website for a quoted fare. A trip from the city centre to the airport will cost around $29 (Dulles), $14 (Reagan National) or $37 (BWI). An up-to-date list of transportation options from Washington's three airports can also be found at www.downtowndc.org/visit/get_around/airports.

Ronald Reagan Washington National Airport

Across the river from DC in Arlington, VA, **Ronald Reagan Washington National Airport** (DCA; ☎ 703-417-8000; www.metwashairports.com) handles domestic services plus some flights to Canada. After a huge renovation a few years back, National was renamed and now contains two fancy terminals (B and C) of shops and restaurants in addition to the original Terminal A. It is easily accessible by Metro (Yellow or Blue Line). The Metro ($1.35) runs from airport concourses B and C and takes about 15 minutes into the city center. A **taxi** (☎ 703-572-8294) to the city center ($12 to $20) took 10 to 30 minutes at the time of research.

Washington Dulles International Airport

Like a space-age castle in the Virginia suburbs, **Washington Dulles International Airport** (IAD; ☎ 703-572-2700; www.metwashairports.com) looms 26 miles west of DC. Take I-66 west to the Dulles Toll Rd. Both domestic and international flights depart from here. Dulles is not on a Metro line, although **Washington Flyer** (☎ 888-927-4359, 703-572-8294;

CLIMATE CHANGE & TRAVEL

Travel – especially air travel – is a significant contributor to global climate change. At Lonely Planet, we believe that all travelers have a responsibility to limit their personal impact. As a result, we have teamed with Rough Guides and other concerned industry partners to support Climate Care, which allows travelers to offset the greenhouse gases they are responsible for with contributions to energy-saving projects and other climate-friendly initiatives in the developing world. Lonely Planet offsets all staff and author travel. For more information, turn to the responsible-travel pages on www.lonelyplanet.com. For details on offsetting your carbon emissions and a carbon calculator, go to www.climatecare.org.

OTHER THAN THE AIRPORT...

Lying as it does at the crossroads of many of the mid-Atlantic's most important overland routes, Washington, DC is better served by rail and bus services than almost any American city but New York. Consider giving some relief to your wallet and the Earth by opting for one of the bus or train options listed below and on p152.

www.washfly.com; round-trip/one way $18/10; 6am-11pm) operates a shuttle from West Falls Church Metro station. The average length of shuttle trips is 20 to 30 minutes. Washington Flyer also operates a door-to-door **taxi service** (703-572-8294); rates depend on distance covered. A one-way taxi trip to the city center (30 to 60 minutes) cost $50 to $55 at the time of research.

Baltimore-Washington International Airport

The **Baltimore-Washington International Airport** (BWI; 800-435-9294; www.bwiairport.com) is 30 miles, or about 45 minutes' drive, northeast of DC in Maryland. Get onto the Baltimore–Washington Parkway via New York Ave NE then follow the parkway until you see the I-195/BWI exit. Often you will find that cheaper airline fares are available to/from BWI than to either National or Dulles, so despite its geographic inconvenience, this is a handy airport for those watching their pennies. A **taxi** (800-878-7743) to the city center cost $90 at the time of research. **Maryland Rail Commuter** (MARC; 800-325-7245, 410-672-6169; www.mtamaryland.com) and Amtrak trains travel between DC's Union Station and a terminal near BWI (weekdays/weekends $7/13), and a Metro-operated **express (B30) bus** (202-637-7000; www.wmata.com/bus/b30_brochure.cfm) runs every 40 minutes between BWI and Greenbelt Metro station.

BUS

The main bus company is **Greyhound** (202-289-5141; www.greyhound.com; 1005 1st St NE), which provides services right across the country. **Peter Pan Trailways** (800-343-9999; www.peterpanbus.com), which travels to northeastern USA, uses a terminal just opposite Greyhound. This run-down neighborhood is deserted after dark, and the nearest Metro station is several blocks south (via 1st St NE) at Union Station. Cabs are usually available at the bus station, and you should definitely use one; don't walk across town from the bus station at night.

Your cheapest option to New York is the Chinatown bus by **New Century Travel** (☎ 202-789-8222; www.2000coach.com; 513 H St NW), which only charges $20 (one way) to get to the Big Apple. The buses are generally clean, and very popular. New Century Travel also operates buses to Philadelphia and Richmond.

TRAIN

Most trains departing Union Station are bound for other East Coast destinations. The station is the southern terminus of the northeast rail corridor, which stops at Baltimore, Philadelphia, New York, New Haven (Connecticut), Boston and intermediate points. There is usually at least one departure per hour throughout the day. Regular (unreserved) trains are cheapest, but pokey. Express Metroliners (reserved) to New York are faster; fastest of all are the fewer-stop Acela trains that zing to New York and on to Boston at speeds in excess of 150mph.

Trains also depart for Virginia destinations (Richmond, Williamsburg, Virginia Beach) and southern destinations, including Florida, New Orleans, Montréal and Amtrak's national hub, Chicago, where you can connect to Midwest– and West Coast–bound trains. MARC and Virginia Railways Express (VRE) commuter trains connect Union Station to Virginia and Maryland.

Fares vary according to type of seating (coach seats or sleeping compartments) and season. Amtrak also offers a variety of all-inclusive holiday tour packages along with regional rail passes and frequent specials.

VISAS

A passport with an official visa is required for most visitors to the United States; contact the American embassy or consulate in your home country for more information on specific requirements. Visitors between the ages of 14 and 79 have to be interviewed before a visa is granted, and all applicants must pay fees that currently stand at $131. You'll also have to prove you're not trying to stay in the USA permanently.

If you are traveling for 90 days or less you may qualify for the Visa Waiver Program (VWP); currently citizens of 43 countries are eligible for this. Learn more at http://travel.state.gov/visa/temp/without/without_1990.html. The Electronic System for Travel Authorization determines if you are eligible for the VWP; its website can be found at https://esta.cbp.dhs.gov. For general visa information, see http://travel.state.gov/visa/temp/types/types_1262.html#6.

GETTING AROUND

More often than not, the best way around DC is by your God-given feet. Almost every neighborhood we've reviewed is supremely walkable, and of course, some spaces, like the Mall, are literally made to be appreciated by pedestrians. With that said, there are some long distances or dodgy neighborhoods that are best covered by the excellent underground Metro system, bus, bicycle or taxi. In this book, the nearest Metro stations are noted after the Ⓜ in each listing. We generally counsel against driving in DC, and our rationale isn't just green (although that is a consideration). Parking is almost always a hassle near major tourist sites and in Georgetown, Adams Morgan, U St, Downtown and Foggy Bottom – garages are expensive and if street spots aren't restricted (and you will get ticketed it you tempt fate), they're usually full, especially on weekend nights. Traffic is often gridlocked during rush hour, and DC's confusing proliferation of one-way streets, roundabouts and where-the-hell-did-that-come-from diagonal avenues (plus aggressive drivers) is generally enough to stretch anyone's sanity.

TRAVEL PASSES

A variety of passes for bus and rail are available, including a one-day pass ($7.80) or a weekly pass ($39).

Transport Times Between Key Destinations

	Smithsonian	Dupont Circle	Metro Center	Georgetown	U Street-Cardozo	Capitol Hill
Smithsonian	n/a	Metro 15min	Metro 5min, walking 15min	bus 30min	Metro or bus 20min	Metro 7min, walking 25min
Dupont Circle	Metro 15min	n/a	Metro 5min	bus 10min	walking 10min	Metro 15-20min
Metro Center	Metro 5min, walking 15min	Metro 5min	n/a	bus 20min	bus 10min, Metro 15min	Metro 10-15min
Georgetown	bus 30min	bus 10min	bus 20min	n/a	bus 40min	bus 30min
U Street-Cardozo	bus or Metro 20min	walking 10min	bus 10min, Metro 15min	bus 40min	n/a	bus or Metro 20min
Capitol Hill	Metro 7min, walking 25min	Metro 15-20min	Metro 10-15min	bus 30min	bus or Metro 20min	n/a

Special passes are available from the **Sales & Information office** (Metro Center station, 12th & F Sts NW), from the website www.wmata.com, and from Safeway and Giant grocery stores.

METRO

DC's sleek modern subway network is the Metrorail, commonly called **Metro** (☎ 202-637-7000; www.wmata.com; fares from $1.35; 5am-midnight Sun-Thu, 5am-3am Fri, 7am-3am Sat, 7am-midnight Sun). It is managed by DC, Maryland, Virginia and the federal government. Thanks to ample federal funding, its trains and stations are well marked, well maintained, well lit, climate controlled, reasonably priced, decently staffed, reliable and safe (if often decked out in ugly orange pleather). Parking is available at certain outlying stations. The distinctive geometric design of the stations is the brainchild of Chicago architect Harry Weese.

To ride Metro, buy a computerized fare card from the self-service machines inside the station entrance. The minimum fare is $1.35, although it increases for longer distances and during rush hour. The posted station-to-station chart provides exact fares for each route. You must use the fare card to enter and exit station turnstiles. Upon exit, the turnstile deducts the fare and returns the card. If the value of the card is insufficient, you need to use an 'Addfare' machine to add money. Other machines inside the gates dispense free bus transfers that enable you to pay just 35¢ on connecting bus routes.

Keep in mind that popular stations such as Smithsonian and Metro Center can get horribly clogged during major events like the Cherry Blossom Festival.

BUS

DC's bus system (technically called 'Metrobus') is operated by the Washington Metropolitan Transit Authority, or Metro. It provides a clean and efficient bus service throughout the city and to outlying suburbs. Stops are marked by red, white and blue signposts. The fare is $1.25 ($3 on express routes), or 35¢ with a Metrorail transfer (available inside Metro stations). Kids under four ride free. Automatic fare machines accept paper dollars, but you must have exact change. Weekly Metrobus passes are a deal at $11.

BICYCLE

Cycling is one of the best ways to get around DC; see p126 for details. In recent years, Metro has taken new measures to encourage bicycle commuting. Riders can take their bikes free of charge on trains, except during rush hours (7am to 10am and 4pm to 7pm Monday to Friday) and on busy holidays, like July 4. Bikes are not permitted to use the center door of trains or the escalator. All buses are now equipped with bike racks, so riders can transport their bikes by bus, too. Here are some options for rental:

Better Bikes Inc (☎ 202-293-2080; www.betterbikesinc.com) Delivers and picks up bikes anywhere in the DC area. Price includes helmets, locks and assistance.

Big Wheel Bikes (☎ 202-337-0254; www.bigwheelbikes.com; 1034 33rd St NW) In Georgetown, just up the hill from the end of the Capital Crescent Trail. Just below M St, look for the bright-yellow building with a huge bicycle on it. There's a three-hour minimum with rentals.

Bike the Sites (☎ 202-842-2453; www.bikethesites.com; 1100 Pennsylvania Ave) Weekly rentals, plus guided tours also available.

Thompson Boat Center (☎ 202-333-9543; www.thompsonboatcenter.com; 2900 Virginia Ave) Easy access to Rock Creek Park and the Capital Crescent Trail. Also, obviously, rents watercraft.

CAR

Rental

All the major car-rental agencies and many small local ones are represented in DC, especially at the airports. Many big agencies maintain offices downtown and at Union Station. Airport rates are often better than those at downtown offices. Car-rental rates do fluctuate radically, but weekly rates are often the best deal. An economy-sized car typically costs $150 to $200 per week. Expect to pay more during peak visitor times, such as the Cherry Blossom Festival, and when big conventions and political demonstrations are in town. The cost of petrol inside the city is more expensive than in neighboring Maryland and Virginia.

Unfortunately for young drivers, most major agencies in DC won't rent to anyone under 25. Some local companies rent to drivers over 21 who have a major credit card, but their rates generally aren't competitive. Agencies in DC include the following:

Alamo (☎ 800-327-9633, 703-260-0182; Dulles airport)

Budget National airport (☎ 703-920-3360); Union Station (☎ 800-527-0700, 202-289-5373)

Enterprise Dulles airport (☎ 703-661-8800); National airport (☎ 703-553-7744); 1029 Vermont Ave NW (☎ 800-325-8007, 202-393-0900)

Hertz National airport (☎ 703-419-6300); Union Station (☎ 202-289-5366)

National Dulles airport (☎ 703-471-5278); National airport (☎ 202-783-1590); Union Station (☎ 888-826-6890, 202-842-7454)

Thrifty Dulles airport and National airport (☎ 877-283-0898); Verizon Center (☎ 202-347-8266)

Share

Zipcar (☎ 866-494-7227; www.zipcar.com), with its cute, eco-friendly Priuses and parking-friendly minis, is a popular commuting tool in this town. If you're on vacation, weekday rates are $9.25/$60 hourly/daily and weekends $10.50/$77. That includes gas and insurance and good parking spaces around town.

TAXI

Taxicabs are plentiful in central DC; hail them with a wave of the hand. **Diamond** (☎ 202-387-4410), **Yellow** (☎ 202-544-1212) and **Capitol** (☎ 202-546-2400) are three major companies. The fare structure has finally graduated from a complicated zone system to normal metered rates – hurrah. Fares generally start at $3.50 at flag drop and increase at roughly 75¢ per half mile – it's a pricey way of getting around. Add at least 10% for the tip and keep in mind that rates increase at night and for radio dispatches. Cabs are easy to hail along major streets and their adjacent arteries, but expect a wait in nightlife hot spots on weekend nights and during major holidays.

PRACTICALITIES

BUSINESS HOURS

Offices generally open between 9am and 5pm, and shops between 10am and 7pm Monday through Saturday and noon to 6pm Sunday (give or take an hour on either side for all of the above). The rather large exception to this is federal government offices, think tanks and associated law firms, NGOs, media outlets etc, where staff may burn the midnight oil throughout the week; with that said, official opening hours adhere to the aforementioned conventions. Bars and clubs are generally open until 1am or 2am on weekdays and 3am on weekends. If you're looking for a visa, embassies have notoriously fickle hours; call or check ahead for each individual country.

CLIMATE

The best time to visit DC is spring (April to May) or autumn (September to October). Summer is a busy tourist season, but weather can be extremely hot and humid, especially in July and August. Plan your travel for the cooler mornings and late afternoons (advance planning can also reduce your time in queues); aim to be inside in air-conditioning during the midday heat; carry water; and wear hats, sunblock and loose, light clothing. Winters are generally mild, with temperatures hovering around freezing. The city has been known to shut down due to snow storms, especially in January.

DANGERS & ANNOYANCES

The nation's capital used to have a notorious reputation for crime, but that reputation has abated to a large degree. Even in the bad old days of the 1980s, this sort of activity was concentrated in poorer neighborhoods and not of a random-attack-on-tourist nature, and as regards current reduced trends, this is still largely the case. Nonetheless, muggings are a reality and you should keep a sensible (but not paranoid) head in areas such as Southeast. Be particularly careful about walking down lonely streets and alleyways in the Adams Morgan and U St neighborhoods on weekend nights; these are popular prowling grounds for muggers. As in all American cities, the emergency line for police, fire and ambulance services is ☎ 911.

ELECTRICITY

Electric current in the USA is 110V to 115V, 60Hz AC. Outlets accept flat two-prong or three-prong grounded plugs. Adapters are available at drugstores, electronics stores and department stores.

EMBASSIES

Almost every country in the world has an embassy in DC, making this one of the US's most vibrant multinational cities. The handy **Electronic Embassy** (www.embassy.org) offers links to all DC embassy homepages. Note that some embassies have outsourced (oh the irony) their visa processing sections to companies such as www.travisa.com; check with individual embassies to see if this is the case.

Australia (Map p63, E3; ☎ 202-797-3000; 1601 Massachusetts Ave NW; M Dupont Circle)
Canada (Map p35, E2; ☎ 202-682-1740; 501 Pennsylvania Ave NW; M Archives-Navy Memorial)
China (☎ 202-328-2500; 2300 Connecticut Ave NW; M Woodley Park-Zoo/Adams Morgan)
France (☎ 202-944-6000; 4101 Reservoir Rd NW; 8:45am-12:45pm; M Georgetown Circulator or shuttle bus)
Germany (☎ 202-298-4000; 4645 Reservoir Rd NW; 8:30-11:30am; M Georgetown Circulator or shuttle bus)
India (☎ 202-939-7000; 2107 Massachusetts Ave NW; M Dupont Circle)
Ireland (☎ 202-462-3939; 2234 Massachusetts Ave NW; M Dupont Circle)
Israel (☎ 202-364-5500; 3514 International Drive NW; M Van Ness-UDC)
Japan (☎ 202-238-6700; 2520 Massachusetts Ave NW; M Dupont Circle)
Mexico (☎ 202-728-1600; 1911 Pennsylvania Ave NW; M Farragut West)
Netherlands (☎ 202-244-5300; 4200 Linnean Ave NW; M Van Ness-UDC)
New Zealand (☎ 202-328-4800; 37 Observatory Circle; N6 from Farragut Sq downtown)
Russia (☎ 202-298-5700; 2650 Wisconsin Ave NW; 30, 32, 34 or 36)
South Africa (☎ 202-232-4400; 3051 Massachusetts Ave NW; N6)
Spain (☎ 202-452-0100; 2375 Pennsylvania Ave NW; M Foggy Bottom-GWU)
UK (☎ 202-588-6500; 3100 Massachusetts Ave NW; N6)

EMERGENCIES

Ambulance/police/fire (☎ 911)
DC Rape Crisis Center (☎ 202-333-7273)
Poison Control (☎ 800-222-1222)
Travelers' Aid Society (☎ 202-546-3120)

HOLIDAYS

Much of Washington, DC shuts down over Christmas and New Year, but other holidays are bustling. The busiest times are spring, especially during the Cherry Blossom Festival and Easter, early summer, the week of Independence Day and Thanksgiving weekend. At these times, expect museums to be packed and prices to be high. Alternatively, during the month of August, and from mid-December to mid-January when Congress is not in session, crowds disappear and bargains abound.

INTERNET

For travelers without a computer, the cheapest place to access the internet is at any branch of the DC public library. Fifteen-minute-limit terminals are available free to the public. If you wish to use the internet for longer than 15 minutes, you must sign up for a user's card, which is also free and allows access to computers at any DC public library. Wi-fi is available in many areas of the city; Tryst (p111) and Busboys & Poets (p84) offer fast, free service. Check www.wififreespot.com/dc for up-to-date listings on other free wi-fi spots. Some good DC web resources:

http://artdc.org Local arts scene.
http://dcist.com Food, events, nightlife.
http://dc.metromix.com More food and fun.
http://wamu.org WAMU, local National Public Radio (NPR) affiliate.
www.culturaltourismdc.org Events, tours and information.
www.dc.gov Local government.
www.dcnites.com Nightlife.
www.downtowndc.org Good gateway.
www.washingtoncitypaper.com *City Paper* – edgy weekly.
www.washington.org Official tourism site with useful links.
www.washingtonpost.com *Washington Post* – broadsheet daily.

MONEY

Most DC businesses accept cash, credit and/or debit cards and traveler's checks; for security and convenience, it is useful to have all three. A credit card may be required for renting a car or making reservations at some hotels. Although the airports have exchange bureaus, better rates can usually be obtained at banks in the city. Some exchange rates are on the inside cover of this guide.

Not counting the cost of your hotel, expect to pay anywhere between $60 and $200 a day in DC, depending on how often you eat out, drink, shop and opt for taxis. If you're truly going budget – self-cooked meals, public transport only and no nightlife – you can scrimp by on a lot less.

American Express (☎ 202-457-1300; 1150 Connecticut Ave NW; Ⓜ Farragut North)

Thomas Cook (☎ 202-237-2229; 5335 Wisconsin Ave NW; Ⓜ Friendship Heights)

TELEPHONE

Pay phones are generally coin operated and it costs 50¢ to make a local call. Prepaid phone cards are sold at newsstands and pharmacies around town. Fax services are available at Kinko's.

USEFUL NUMBERS

All numbers in this book are presented with area codes – either DC's (☎ 202) or another area. Other useful numbers:

Directory assistance (☎ 411)
International operator (☎ 00)
Maryland area codes (☎ 301, 410, 443)
Operator (☎ 0)
Toll-free prefixes (☎ 800, 888)
US country code (☎ 1)
Virginia area codes (☎ 703, 571)

TIPPING

Gratuities are not optional in the US. Waitstaff, hotel-room attendants, valet parkers and bellhops receive the minimum wage or less and depend on tips for their livelihoods. Service has to be pretty dreadful before you should consider not tipping. In restaurants tipping 15% of the total bill is the accepted minimum. If service is good, 20% is a decent average tip; give more if service is exceptional. Hotel-room attendants should get $1 per guest per day, eg $10 for two people who have stayed five days. Tip taxi drivers about 10% of your fare. Airport baggage handlers get about $1 per bag. Hairdressers usually get tips (20%), as do coat-check staff ($1).

TOURIST INFORMATION

Washington, DC operates several information centers in the city to help travelers arrange accommodation and develop itineraries.

DC Chamber of Commerce Visitor Information Center (☎ 202-328-4748; www.dcchamber.org; 1300 Pennsylvania Ave NW, Ronald Reagan Bldg; 🕑 8am-4:30pm Mon-Fri Sep 2-Mar 14, 8:30am-5:30pm Mon-Fri, 9am-4pm Sat Mar 15-Sep 1; Ⓜ Federal Triangle) Offers tours, maps, lodging brochures and events listings, and sells film, tickets and souvenirs.

NPS Ellipse Visitor Pavilion (☎ 202-208-1631; 🕑 8am-3pm) At the northeast corner of the Ellipse, south of the White House.

Smithsonian Visitors Center (☎ 202-633-1000, 202-633-5285; www.si.edu/visit; 1000 Jefferson Dr SW, Smithsonian Institution Building, The Castle; 🕑 8:30am-5:30pm Mon-Sat; Ⓜ Smithsonian) Everything you ever wanted to know about the museum programs.

Washington DC Convention & Visitors Association (☎ 202-789-7000; www.washington.org; 901 7th St NW, 4th fl; 🕑 9am-5pm Mon-Fri; Ⓜ Metro Center) Distributes information by mail on lodgings, restaurants and attractions, or you can visit its office.

TRAVELERS WITH DISABILITIES

DC is an excellent destination for visitors with disabilities. Most museums and major sights are wheelchair accessible, as are most large hotels and restaurants. The **Smithsonian** (☎ 202-633-1000, TTY 202-357-1729) and many other museums arrange special tours for people with visual, auditory or other impairments.

All Metro trains and most buses are wheelchair accessible. All Metro stations have elevators, and guide dogs are allowed on trains and buses. People with disabilities who can't use public transit can use **MetroAccess** (☎ 301-562-5360), a door-to-door transport provider. Many large hotels have suites for disabled guests, but call the hotel itself – not the chain's 800 number – to check before you reserve. Larger car-rental agencies offer hand-controlled models at no extra charge. All major airlines, Greyhound buses and Amtrak trains allow service animals on board and frequently sell two-for-one packages if you need an attendant to accompany you.

Out of doors, hindrances to wheelchair users include buckled-brick sidewalks in the historic blocks of Georgetown and Capitol Hill, but sidewalks in most other parts of DC are in good shape and have dropped curbs. Unfortunately, only a handful of crosswalks, mostly near the Mall, have audible crossing signals. Hearing-impaired visitors should check out **Gallaudet University** (☎ 202-651-5000; www.gallaudet.edu) in Northeast DC, which hosts lectures and cultural events especially for the deaf.

>INDEX

See also separate subindexes for Drink (p166), Eat (p166), Play (p167), See (p167) and Shop (p168).

000 map pages

DRINK

000 map pages

EAT

SHOP

000 map pages